BEST OF

Rome

KU-209-831

Abigail Hole

Colour-Coding & Maps

Each chapter has a colour code along the banner at the top of the page which is also used for text and symbols on maps (eg all venues reviewed in the Highlights chapter are orange on the maps). The fold-out maps inside the front and back covers are numbered from 1 to 6. All sights and venues in the text have map references; eg, (4, F3) means Map 4, grid reference F3. See p128 for map symbols.

Prices

Multiple prices listed with reviews (eg €10/5) usually indicate adult/concession admission to a venue. Concession prices can include senior, student, member or coupon discounts. Meal cost and room rate categories are listed at the start of the Eating and Sleeping chapters, respectively.

Text Symbols

- ☎ telephone
- ⊠ address
- 🖳 email/website address
- € admission
- ☽ opening hours
- ⓘ information
- Ⓜ metro
- 🚍 bus
- 🚋 tram/cable car/trolley
- Ⓟ parking available
- ⓑ wheelchair access
- ⊠ on site/nearby eatery
- 🧒 child-friendly venue
- Ⓥ good vegetarian selection

Best of Rome
3rd edition – September 2006
First published – June 2001

Published by Lonely Planet Publications Pty Ltd
ABN 36 005 607 983

Australia Head Office, Locked Bag 1, Footscray, Vic 3011
  ☎ 03 8379 8000, fax 03 8379 8111
  🖳 talk2us@lonelyplanet.com.au
USA 150 Linden St, Oakland, CA 94607
  ☎ 510 893 8555, toll free 800 275 8555
  fax 510 893 8572
  🖳 info@lonelyplanet.com
UK 72–82 Rosebery Ave, Clerkenwell, London EC1R 4RW
  ☎ 020 7841 9000, fax 020 7841 9001
  🖳 go@lonelyplanet.co.uk

This title was commissioned in Lonely Planet's London office and produced by: **Commissioning Editors** Paula Hardy, Tasmin McNaughtan **Coordinating Editor** Katie Lynch **Coordinating Cartographers** Emma McNicol, Valentina Kremenchutskaya **Layout Designer** David Kemp **Proofer** Craig Kilburn **Managing Cartographer** Mark Griffiths **Managing Editor** Brigitte Ellemor **Cover Designer** Annika Roojun **Project Manager** Rachel Imeson **Language Content Coordinator** Quentin Frayne **Thanks to** Sally Darmody, Celia Wood, Trent Paton

Photographs by Martin Moos/Lonely Planet Images except for the following: p5, 51 Witold Skrypczak/Lonely Planet Images, p26 Australian Picture Library/Corbis/George Tatge, p41 Jonathan Smith/Lonely Planet Images, p52 Australian Picture Library/Corbis/Sandro Vannini, p81 Oliver Strewe/Lonely Planet Images, p82 Jerry Alexander/Lonely Planet Images, p86 John Neubauer/Lonely Planet Images, p87 Krzysztof Dydynski/Lonely Planet Images. **Cover photograph** Fernando Santis in front of a *pizzicheria* (delicatessen), Photolibrary/Agefotostock. All images are copyright of the photographers unless otherwise indicated. Many of the images in this guide are available for licensing from Lonely Planet Images: www.lonelyplanetimages.com.

ISBN 1 74059 736 2

Printed through Colorcraft Ltd, Hong Kong.
Printed in China

Acknowledgments Rome Metro Map © 2006 ATAC S.p.A

Contents

From the Publisher

AUTHOR
Abigail Hole

Several years ago Abigail came to Rome for a month, and liked it so much she stayed. She lives here with her Italian partner and son, who was born in Rome. She is a freelance travel journalist who has also lived in London and Hong Kong; other favourite Lonely Planet assignments have included India, Mali, Mauritania, Egypt and Portugal.

Special thanks to Luca, Gabriel, Marina, Nicola and the many people who helped me out with recommendations, especially Ben, Paola (and friends), Sandro, Maria Rita, Sylvia, Karola, Stephanie, Marco and Phil. Thanks to Isabella and Valentina for help with museum research. *Tante grazie a Anna, Marcello, Mum e Ant per il loro lavoro di babysitting.* Thanks also to Paula, Michala and Tasmin at Lonely Planet.

LONELY PLANET AUTHORS
Why is our travel information the best in the world? It's simple: our authors are independent, dedicated travellers. They don't research using just the Internet or phone, and they don't take freebies in exchange for positive coverage. They travel widely, to all the popular spots and off the beaten track. They personally visit thousands of hotels, restaurants, cafés, bars, galleries, palaces, museums and more – and they take pride in getting all the details right, and telling it how it is. For more, see the authors section on **www.lonelyplanet.com**.

PHOTOGRAPHER
Martin Moos

Born in Zürich, Switzerland, Martin got the obvious banking degree before escaping onto the travellers' trail with his Nikon gear in 1986. Seven years in Northeast Asia provided oodles of motives for an in-depth learning-by-doing. Martin is presently based again in Zürich, together with his wife and two children, cramped by mountains of slides.

SEND US YOUR FEEDBACK
We love to hear from travellers – your comments keep us on our toes and help make our books better. Our well-travelled team reads every word on what you loved or loathed about this book. Although we cannot reply individually to postal submissions, we always guarantee that your feedback goes straight to the appropriate authors, in time for the next edition – and the most useful submissions are rewarded with a free book. To send us your updates – and find out about Lonely Planet events, newsletters and travel news – visit our award-winning website: **www.lonelyplanet.com/feedback**.

Note: We may edit, reproduce and incorporate your comments in Lonely Planet products such as guidebooks, websites and digital products, so let us know if you don't want your comments reproduced or your name acknowledged. For a copy of our privacy policy visit **www.lonelyplanet.com/privacy**.

Introducing Rome

Its *caput mundi* – capital of the world – days may be over, but Rome is still the world's greatest capital. It's cityscape as theatre, filled with monumental spectacle. Here history thrusts through the walls of the present, but it's not a heritage city pandering to the past: it's chaotic, relaxed and frantic, filled to the brim with its stylish, traditional, anarchic, conformist, self-centred, charming and ebullient inhabitants.

The Romans live nonchalantly among great imperial ruins, exposed or incorporated into the city. Then there are the baroque spectaculars – public spaces created for the utmost impact: Piazza Navona, once an ancient stadium, or the Fontana di Trevi, filling an entire square with foaming, fantastical figures, or St Peter's piazza – a colonnaded embrace. Built across seven hills, the city also has a feast of views. The spires and domes of Christianity's capital create an ochre-and-orange skyline, puncturing a usually blue sky (the climate is good too – after all, Rome's home to the Pope).

So there's a lot to see, but make time for idling in sunbathed cafés, getting lost in narrow cobbled streets, and whiling away hours at local *trattorie*. Rome is so packed with wonders, be they ancient Roman, Renaissance or baroque (and often all three rolled into one), that they appear around every corner, even if you don't seek them out.

Bernini's extraordinary St Peter's Square (p9)

Neighbourhoods

Despite being definitely not built in a day, Rome is an astonishingly manageable city. You can walk much of it, using the occasional bus or metro hop for further-flung sights.

Major highlights are mostly within walking distance of the **centro storico** (historic city centre), defined by the Tiber river to the west, Villa Borghese to the north, the Roman Forum to the south and Stazione Termini to the east. This encompasses the Pantheon, Piazza Navona, the Ghetto, Piazza del Popolo, and Tridente, with lots of baroque gems, designer shops, boutiques, cafés and restaurants.

Ancient Rome appears everywhere, lying as it does beneath the layers of the medieval, Renaissance and modern city, but its glories are concentrated around the **Capitoline** and **Palatine hills** – the Roman Forum, the Palatine and the Colosseum.

North of the Colosseum lie mixed-bag **Monti** and **Esquilino** districts. Within these, a trendy sliver of **Cavour** is home to some boho bars and boutiques, while east lies **Termini**, Rome's main railway hub, faintly sleazy and with many cheap hotels. Further east still is the happening university district **San Lorenzo**.

OFF THE BEATEN TRACK

There's so much to see in Rome, it's easy to find places not overrun with other travellers. Head to the parks and gardens (p42), or lovely Aventino (p44 and p33), visit Keats and co at the non-Catholic cemetery, Cimitero Acattolico per gli Stranieri (p38), or quieter museums and sights like Palazzo Altemps (p29), Casa di Goethe (p27), Centrale Montemartini (p27) and the Galeria Doria Pamphilj (p26). San Lorenzo (p93), the student district, and the *centri sociali* (social centre; see the boxed text, p93) have a lively nighttime off-beat buzz.

Chilling out in Palazzo Altemps

St Peter's Basilica, the **Vatican City** and genteel **Borgo** and **Prati** districts lie on the Tiber's west bank, as does **Trastevere**, one of Rome's most beguiling areas, with labyrinthine lanes lined with restaurants, bars and bonhomie.

South of Trastevere is beautiful **Aventino**, a stately residential area, while just south of here lies **Testaccio**, sometime working-class, now edgily trendy and a nightlife centre. Its trendiness is seeping over into neighbouring **Ostiense**, whose main focus was once Rome's wholesale fruit and veg market. Further south beyond Ostiense lies the Fascist architecture of middle-class **EUR**.

The huge defensive wall you'll spot encircling the centre was built in the 3rd century by Emperor Aurelian and strengthened by medieval popes.

Itineraries

The saying goes: *Roma, non basta una vita* (Rome, a lifetime is not enough), but your visit will probably be somewhat shorter. If you've only got a few days, use this book's Highlights to sift through the city's major sights.

It's amazing how much you can see by wandering through the *centro storico* (historic city centre). You could fit several highlights into one day, though the glorious Vatican easily deserves a day on its own. Pepper your sightseeing with leisurely lunches and strong coffees to recharge your batteries. Sights like the Colosseum are always busy, but you can change pace by ambling around the Palatine or Villa Borghese, and there are many museums you'll have almost to yourself, no matter how magnificent their contents.

ROME LOWLIGHTS
Some things make Rome 'eternal' for all the wrong reasons:
- Traffic, pollution, mad driving, parking
- Grumpy shop 'assistants'
- Rip-off eateries around major sights
- All those camera-clicking tourists!
- Roving vendors

Arco di Tito at the Roman Forum (p8)

DAY ONE

Walk up to the Capitoline and Michelangelo's piazza, visit the museums and have lunch at their café. Gasp at the view of the Roman Forum and then wander through its ruins and visit the Palatine, the Colosseum or San Clemente. Make a night of it in lively, lovely Trastevere.

DAY TWO

Start off at the Vatican and St Peter's, then allow yourself a long lunch: you've earned it. Heading back to the historical centre, it's time for a leisurely wander through Piazza Navona and over to the Pantheon. Head back to 'Il Campo' for fun after dark.

DAY THREE

Immerse yourself in Roman life at the market in Campo de' Fiori before zipping up to Villa Borghese and Galleria Borghese. After lunch in Tridente, spruce up your wardrobe at the swish designer stores around Via Condotti in preparation for your evening stroll. Try to make it to Palazzo Massimo Alle Terme before heading out for the nightlife around Piazza Navona.

Campo de' Fiori (p41) living up to its name

Highlights

ROMAN FORUM (4, H6)

Before you do anything, stand on Capitoline Hill overlooking this astonishing site.

Just a typical 'piazza' in the Republic's early days, the Forum became gradually surrounded by gleaming white marble law courts, offices and temples. It's bisected by the cobbled and ceremonial **Via Sacra** (Sacred Way). The elaborate **Arco di Settimio Severo** (AD 203) celebrates Roman victory over the Parthians. To the right are the **Rostrum** ruins – here Shakespeare's Mark Antony asked all present to lend him their ears. Nearby is **Basilica Giulia**, built by Julius Caesar – whose remains were cremated here – and completed by Augustus. Behind it was **Casa delle Vestali**, home of the Vestal virgins, who chastely (those who broke their vows were buried alive) kept the sacred flame alight. At the Colosseum end is the **Arco di Tito** built in AD 81 to honour victories of Titus against the Jews, with friezes showing armies looting Jerusalem. Nearby is the mammoth **Basilica of Maxentius**, once a gilded meeting hall measuring 65m by 100m.

INFORMATION
- ☎ 06 3996 7700
- ✉ entrances at Largo Romolo e Remo 5-6, Piazza di Santa Maria Nova 53 & Via di Monte Tarpeo
- € admission free
- ☼ 9am-1hr before dusk
- ⓘ audiotour €4 from Palatine ticket office
- 🚌 to Via dei Fori Imperiali or Piazza Venezia
- Ⓜ Colosseo
- ♿ limited
- ✗ see p77

DON'T MISS
- View over the Forum at dusk
- Marble friezes inside the Curia (where the Senate met) showing a snapshot of Forum life
- Marks on the steps of Basilica Giulia – the remains of ancient idlers' games

The Forum crumbled as the empire fell. Ravaged by barbarians and builders, it was nicknamed the Campus Vaccinus (cow field) in medieval times. Excavations began in the 19th century, and what you see now is 1400 to 2500 years old. To unscramble the stones, get an audio tour from the ticket office.

Evidence of past glories – the Roman Forum

ST PETER'S BASILICA (4, A3)

The mighty magnificence of St Peter's is everything you might expect from the capital of Christendom. Obviously no one informed its builders that the meek will inherit the earth.

Seventeenth-century St Peter's Square is an extraordinary public arena, embraced by two colonnades, overseen by 140 saints. Bernini planned the piazza to be a surprise after the tangle of medieval streets, an effect spoilt by Mussolini who bulldozed a massive approach road.

St Peter was martyred near here in the 1st century and in 315 Constantine built a basilica on the site of his tomb. The original was on the verge of collapse when Pope Julius II commissioned Renaissance architects – including Bramante and Raphael – to build anew. But Michelangelo gets most of the credit and his astonishing **dome**, completed in 1590 (well after his death) is an incredible 119m high. Maderno extended the nave in the early 17th century to form a Latin cross and built the façade, adorned with huge statues of Christ and the apostles.

Papal tombs crowd the basement, including John Paul II's tomb. The vast interior, with a capacity of 60,000, is imposing rather than beautiful; this is the world's second biggest church (the largest is in Yamoussoukro, Ivory Coast).

The highlight is Michelangelo's moving *Pietà*, sculpted when he was just 25. Other treasures include Bernini's *Throne of St Peter* and the Alexander VII monument. But Bernini's cherub-topped **baldacchino**, made with Pantheon bronze, dominates. Soaring 29m above the pope's high altar, it is believed to stand over the exact site of St Peter's grave.

INFORMATION

- ☎ infoline 06 6988 37 12, Vatican Necropolis 06 698 73 017
- 🖳 www.vatican.va
- ✉ Piazza San Pietro
- € admission free; dome with/ without lift €7/4
- ☽ basilica 7am-6pm (7am-7pm Apr-Sep), dome 8am-5pm (8am-6pm Apr-Sep)
- ⓘ dress appropriately: covered shoulders, no shorts
- 🚌 to Piazza del Risorgimento
- Ⓜ Ottaviano
- ♿ good
- ✂ see p80

DON'T MISS

- Climbing up 550 steps to the dome summit (you can get the lift half-way)
- The toe on the bronze statue of St Peter, worn down by centuries of pilgrims' kisses
- The carved face of a woman giving birth at the baldacchino's base
- Giotto's *Navicella* in the entrance
- Bronze floor plates showing the next biggest churches

SISTINE CHAPEL & VATICAN MUSEUMS (4, B2, A2)

You could fall over backwards wondering at the **Sistine Chapel**, enveloped by Renaissance works of genius. Muscular figures pound out of their two dimensions, interspersed by blazing heavenly blue. Fifteenth-century masterpieces cover the walls, including works by Botticelli, Ghirlandaio, Pinturicchio and Signorelli. All spectacularly eclipsed by a man who didn't even consider himself a painter.

Jealous rivals encouraged Julius II to commission Michelangelo, hoping that out of his element, he would fail (see the boxed text, p109). At first reluctant, Michelangelo responded by providing much more than was asked, covered the ceiling (1508–12) with incredible renderings of Genesis. Twenty years later, he was invited back to paint the altar wall, outdoing himself with the harsher, more naked Last Judgement (1541). Not everyone was in awe however; Pius IV ordered fig leaves and loin clothes painted on the dangly bits. Both works were controversially restored recently, and now are as vibrant as the day Michelangelo took down the scaffolding.

Since the 16th century, the College of Cardinals holes up here when required to elect a new pope. Progress is indicated by smoke from the chimney; black indicating no result, white heralding a decision. In 2005 the world held its breath after the death of John Paul II and watched the chimney. Puffs of black smoke showed the cardinals were having trouble making their minds up, before white smoke heralded the choice of German traditionalist Joseph Ratzinger – now Pope Benedict XVI.

The **Vatican Museums** are not just about the magnificent Sistine Chapel. This collection of museums feels like an endless, magical palace, where wonderment can fast turn to museum-induced irritable exhaustion.

If you don't have the luxury of several visits, head for the Sistine Chapel, the Stanze di Raffaello and the Pinoteca. The complex is exceptionally organised, with several routes taking from 45 minutes to five hours.

INFORMATION

- ☎ 06 698 83 333
- 🖳 www.vatican.va
- ✉ Viale del Vaticano
- € adult/concession €12/7, free last Sun of month
- ☾ 8.45am-1.45pm Mon-Fri early Jan-early Mar & Nov-late Dec, 8.45am-4.45pm Mon-Fri, 8.45am-1.45pm Sat early Mar-Oct & late Dec-early Jan, 8.45am-1.45pm last Sun of month; last admission 1½hr before close
- ⓘ CD 1½-hr audio guides €6
- 🚌 to Piazza del Risorgimento
- Ⓜ Ottaviano, Cipro-Musei Vaticani
- ♿ excellent
- ✖ see p80

More colours than you can poke a lance at – a Swiss guard at the Vatican

MEET THE POPE

On Wednesday at 11am the Pope meets his flock at St Peter's (in July and August at Castelgandolfo). To attend, write to the Prefettura della Casa Pontificia, 00120 Città del Vaticano. If you're already in Rome, call or visit the Prefettura (☎ 06 69 88 46 31; ☻ 9am-1pm) through the bronze doors under the colonnade right of St Peter's.

Don't forget to look up – the ceiling of Galleria delle Carte Geografiche at the Vatican Museums

The **Stanze di Raffaello** are Pope Julius II's splendid private apartments, which Raphael diligently decorated as Michelangelo toiled along the corridor. His outstanding work, *School of Athens,* represents all human knowledge, featuring philosophers, scholars and artists, including Michelangelo (the lone foreground figure) and himself (second from right).

Nearby, don't overlook the meek Fra Angelico **Chapel of Nicholas V,** with scenes from the lives of saints Stephen and Lawrence.

The **Pinacoteca** is chock-a-block with paintings by Giotto (check out the Stefaneschi Altarpiece), Caravaggio, Leonardo da Vinci, Filippo Lippi, Federico Barocci, Guido Reni, Guercino, Nicolas Poussin, van Dyck, Pietro da Cortona, more Raphael, and many others.

Beautiful **Galleria delle Carte Geografiche** has 40 exquisite topographical maps and 16th-century frescoes of Italian regions.

Museo Pio-Clementino exhibits masterpieces of classical sculpture such as the marble *Apollo Belvedere,* a Roman copy of a 4th-century-BC Greek bronze, the iconic Graeco-Romano marble *Laocoön* (150 BC), which influenced Michelangelo, and the anatomic ideal of the *Belvedere torso.*

Elsewhere in the complex, fascinating Egyptian treasures are found in **Museo Gregoriano Egizio**. Etruscan wares, including stunning gold jewellery and terracotta portraits, are showcased in **Museo Gregoriano Etrusco**. Here you can also glimpse Bramante's staircase, large enough for visitors on horseback. **Museo Pio-Cristiano** features early Christian antiquities (mainly from the Catacombs), and there's Pagan Greek and Roman statuary aplenty in **Museo Gregoriano Profano**.

DON'T MISS

- Raphael's *Trasfigurazione,* Leonardo's unfinished *San Gerolamo,* Caravaggio's *Deposition,* Pinacoteca
- Fra Angelico frescoes, Pope Nicholas V's private chapter

COLOSSEUM (4, H6)

Size, splendour and sheer goriness continue to pull the crowds into the Colosseum. From AD 80 battles between gladiators, wild animals, slaves and other unlucky folk entertained 50,000 bloodthirsty Romans. Standing in its barren interior – a blueprint for today's stadia – you can imagine the roar of the crowd.

Gladiators were professionals and sometimes spared if they'd put up a good enough scrap (they could appeal to the presiding VIP), but not so the unfortunate opponents. Their corpses were prodded with red-hot irons to ensure they weren't 'playing dead'.

In Christian Rome, gladiatorial games were banned in AD 438, and hunting in AD 523. With the fall of the Empire, the Colosseum was abandoned and became a quarry for building materials – the pitted holes in the exterior were left when its metal cramps were looted – and became overgrown with exotic plants, seeds of which had been transported by the wild beasts that perished here. In the middle ages two of Rome's foremost families converted it into a fortress, but the damage only really stopped when a mid-18th century pope consecrated the site as a church.

The broken interior provides the opportunity to see spooky subterranean tunnels where animals and combatants cowered prior to their debuts.

Guides here are usefully amplified so you can dip in and out of passing tours. Buy your ticket at the Palatine ticket office to avoid colossal queues.

INFORMATION

- ☎ 06 399 67 700
- 🖥 booking www.pierreci.it
- ✉ Piazza del Colosseo
- € adult/concession €10/5 (includes Palatine)
- 🕐 9am-6.30pm, last exit 7.30pm
- Ⓜ Colosseo
- ♿ fair
- ✗ see p77

COLOSSAL GORE

To celebrate the Colosseum's inauguration, Titus (79–81) held games that lasted 100 days, during which 5000 animals died. Trajan (98–117) topped this, holding a 117-day long killing spree to celebrate victory in Dacia (present-day Romania), involving 9000 gladiators and 10,000 animals.

VILLA & GALLERIA BORGHESE (3, C3)

Baroque playground of Rome's most illustrious family, Villa Borghese was built by Cardinal Scipione Borghese to house his outstanding art collection, which was gathered by flexing his political muscles.

The rambling parklands, with formal gardens, lakes, temples and summerhouses, are a wonderful place for a stroll or cycle (bike hire available), and contain Bioparco (p44), Museo Canonica (p28), Teatro Silvano Toti Globe (p87) and the charming, tethered hot-air balloon for 150m-high city views.

Seventeenth-century Galleria Borghese's interior resembles a jewellery box. The lower floor contains exquisite 4th-century mosaics, Canova's daring sculpture of a topless Paolina Bonaparte Borghese (Napoleon's sister), and spectacular sculptures by the young Bernini. See Pluto's hand pressing into Proserpine's thigh in the dramatic *Rape of Proserpine*, the transforming nymph and Apollo's slow realisation in *Apollo and Daphne*, and compare Bernini's dynamic *David* with Michelangelo's languorous version.

You will also find an unparalleled six Caravaggios, including the arresting *Madonna with the Serpent*, snapped up after rejection

INFORMATION

- ☎ gallery 06 328 10; balloon 045860 11 99
- 🖳 gallery www.galleriaborghese .it, booking www.ticketeria.it; balloon www.aerophile.it
- ✉ park entrances at Porta Pinciana, Piazzale Flaminio & Pincio; gallery Piazzale del Museo Borghese
- € adult/concession €8.50/5.25
- ⓘ gallery admittance restricted at peak times – it may pay to book; English 2hr guided tour 9.10am, €5
- ☽ park sunrise-sunset; gallery 9am-7pm Tue-Sun
- 🚌 Via Vittorio Veneto or Piazzale Flaminio
- ♿ good
- 🍽 museum café

A Caravaggiophile's delight

DON'T MISS

- Hot-air balloon
- The view from Pincio
- *Sleeping Hermaphrodite*
- Pietro Bernini's bas-relief of horse and rider
- 16th-century erotica: Correggio's *Danae*
- Fra Bartolomeo's beautiful *Adoration of Christ Child*
- Perugino's *Madonna with Child*

by ecclesiastical commissioners, *Sick Bacchus*, possibly a selfportrait, and *David with the head of Goliath* (painted after Caravaggio's banishment from Rome to show how sorry he was).

The **Pinacoteca** is crowded with masterpieces, including Raphael's *Deposition* and *Susanna and the Elders*, Titian's *Venus Blindfolding Cupid* and *Sacred and Profane Love*, Rubens' *Pietà* and Cranach's *Venus and Cupid with Honeycomb*.

CAPITOLINE HILL (2, C1)

Capitoline Hill was ancient Rome's most sacred place, where all ceremonial processions ended. It was topped by two temples – to Jupiter Capitolinus, and to Juno Moneta, housing the Roman mint (hence the word 'money'), where Santa Maria in Aracoeli (p35) now stands.

INFORMATION

- ✉ Piazza del Campidoglio
- 🚌 to Piazza Venezia (6, F3)
- ♿ excellent (access via road to right of La Cordonata)
- ✘ see p70

The hill is topped by Michelangelo's **Piazza del Campidoglio**, arguably the world's most perfect public space, like an elegant outdoor ballroom.

The most impressive approach is via **La Cordonata**, a stepped ramp that sweeps up from Piazza Venezia and gently conveys its cargo in between two mammoth Roman statues of Castor and Pollux, the twin saviours of Rome, and on to the piazza. In the centre gallops a **statue of Marcus Aurelius** (who ruled AD 161–180) – a copy. The original, in the Palazzo Nuovo, is the only equestrian bronze surviving from ancient Rome. It was spared medieval meltdown because it was mistakenly identified as Constantine, the first Christian emperor. Michelangelo had it transferred here from San Giovanni in Laterano, Rome's first Christian basilica.

Michelangelo also designed or remodelled the piazza's three *palazzi*. Facing the steps is the Palazzo Senatorio, modern Rome's city hall. The **Palazzo Nuovo** and the **Palazzo dei Conservatori** house the outstanding **Capitoline Museums** (see opposite).

WHO'S WHO AT THE CAMPIDOGLIO

Sitting at either side of the steps, Castor and Pollux were twins born to Leda and a swan (Jupiter in disguise). Disguised as knights, they told the Romans that they'd win the battle of Regillus (499 BC) and were hence thought of as Rome's saviours.

Across the square is a 1st-century BC statue of Minerva, their divine sister, with the Tiber to her right and the Nile on the left.

Michelanglo's perfect Piazza del Campidoglio

CAPITOLINE MUSEUMS (2, C1)

Ancient Rome's finest treasures lie in these palaces. These are the world's oldest public museums, founded in 1471 when Pope Sixtus IV donated a few sculptures to the city, and added to by successive popes.

Palazzo dei Conservatori contains the remarkable frescoed **Hall of the Orazi and Curiazi**, with surreal fragments of the 4th-century colossal bronze of Constantine that originally stood at the Forum, and a gilded 2nd-century bronze of Hercules, overlooked by Bernini's blustering sculpture of Pope Urban VIII.

You will also find the famous 6th-century BC Etruscan bronze *She-wolf* (with suckling Renaissance twins) and the captivating 1st-century-BC *Spinario,* a rare original Greek bronze.

The **Pinacoteca**, upstairs, brims with masterpieces including Caravaggio's naughty-looking *St John the Baptist,* Tintoretto's distraught *Penitent Magdelene* and Titian's *Baptism of Christ.*

You can cross to the other *palazzo* via the square or through the artefact-lined tunnel, via the **Tabularium**, home to Roman funerary inscriptions – touching memorials to ancient loved ones.

Palazzo Nuovo is filled with busts that provide a veritable who's who of ancient Rome. The most important sculptures are the restored

INFORMATION

- ☎ 06 399 67 800
- 🖥 www.museicapitolini.org
- ✉ Piazza del Campidoglio
- € adult/concession €6.20/4.20, tickets are valid all day
- 🕐 9am-8pm Tue-Sun
- 🚌 to Piazza Venezia (6, F3)
- ♿ excellent (access via road to right of La Cordonata)
- 🍴 museum café

You'll be statued out after a Capitoline visit

DON'T MISS

- The room containing 67 Caesars
- The magnificent view of the Forum from the Tabularium
- Guercino's huge Santa Petronilla altarpiece
- The museum café, with superb views
- The Capitoline overflow at Centrale Montmartini (see p27)

Marcus Aurelius (a copy stands in the piazza), the poignant *Dying Galatian,* a Roman copy of a 3rd-century-BC Greek, the sensual 1st-century-BC *Capitoline Venus* with breasts that seem stuck on, and a *Satyr Resting,* which inspired Nathanial Hawthorne's book, the *Marble Faun.* There's also an amazing dove mosaic from Hadrian's villa, so fine it resembles a painting.

SAN CLEMENTE (5, A6)

This is Rome's most extraordinary church. To visit is a voyage of discovery: a 12th-century basilica, built over a 4th-century church, built over a 1st-century Roman house that contained a 2nd-century pagan temple. Bring a torch to illuminate the corners.

Best entered through the medieval courtyard, the church is dominated by a glimmering 12th-century mosaic showing the Triumph of the Cross. Masolino decorated the chapel of St Catherine, possibly assisted by his brilliant student, Masaccio. Renaissance frescoes recount scenes from the saint's life, who was eventually strapped to a wheel and tortured to death (after all that she had the honour of having a firework named after her).

INFORMATION

- ☎ 06 704 51 018
- ✉ Via di San Giovanni in Laterano
- € admission free, crypt €3
- ⏱ 9am-12.30pm & 3-6pm Mon-Sat, 10am-12.30pm & 3-6pm Sun
- 🚌 🚋 Via Labicana
- Ⓜ Colosseo
- ♿ limited (access to medieval church only)
- ✗ see p77

A glittering 12th-century mosaic at Basilica di San Clemente

DON'T MISS

- Magnificent Cosmati floor mosaics
- 6th-century marble choir
- Cosmati Paschal candlestick
- Unfinished Roman sarcophagi embedded in the stair walls – faces would've been added after they were sold

Below the 12th-century basilica lies the **4th-century church**, resembling a huge arched granary. It was decimated by Norman invaders in 1084, but you can study stunning, faded 11th-century frescoes illustrating St Clemente's life and many miracles.

Descend another level into an ancient Roman lane leading to a 1st-century house with buckling floors and the dank, mystical **Temple of Mithras**, containing an otherworldly altar that depicts Mithras slaying a bull. Mithaism was a Persian, men-only cult.

And there are still more layers beneath this. The sound of rushing water is an underground river flowing through a Republican-era drain to feed the Tiber.

PALAZZO MASSIMO ALLE TERME (5, A3)

Don't miss this museum's extraordinary treasures – marvellous Ancient Roman artefacts, mosaics, and fresco decorations for entire rooms.

The basement houses a surprisingly fascinating coin collection. Currency glints like chocolate money, and intelligent displays show how coinage was used as propaganda. Also on show is exquisite good-as-new Roman jewellery, and silver cups with itineraries inscribed on them – Roman souvenirs.

Early Republican age sculpture fills the ground floor, with portraits supplying a sense of the Roman physiognomy. There are also some rare Greek originals, including a superb 5th-century-BC sculpture of Noibid extracting an arrow from her back.

Up a level and you'll find sculpture from the Flavian era, including the perfect *Sleeping Hermaphrodite*, showing the ancient fascination with ambivalent sexuality, and 5th-century copies of the famous Greek *Discus Thrower*. Busts of high-class Roman women show the evolution of ancient hairstyles, and there are bronzes that were found in Nemi lake – relics from boats that floated opposite Caligula's lakeside villa – including an elegant balustrade.

It gets even better on the 2nd floor, with entire rooms of frescoes. What was a sunken room (to beat the summer heat) in Casa di Livia – possibly home to Augustus and his wife – is decorated as a Mediterranean garden, and there are beautiful small Villa della Farnesina bedrooms. The mosaics on this floor are remarkable, and there's some rare, glinting inlaid work.

DON'T MISS
- The statue of Augustus as Pontifex Maximus
- Portrait head of Livia
- Terracotta artefacts from the Palatine's Domus Tiberiana
- The bedrooms of Villa Farnesina on the 2nd floor
- The bookshop

INFORMATION
- ☎ 06 3996 7700
- ✉ Largo di Villa Peretti 1
- € adult/concession €9/6, includes Palazzo Altemps, Crypta Balbi & Terme di Diocleziano, valid three days; audio guide €7
- ☺ 9am-7.45pm Tue-Sun
- Ⓜ Termini, Repubblica
- ♿ excellent
- ✄ see p81

Treasure-filled Palazzo Massimo alla Terme

PANTHEON (6, C2)

The Pantheon is ancient Rome's best-preserved edifice. It's unlike any other building.

Eighteen monolithic Corinthian columns line the grim, solid façade. Marks in the columns were made when the portico was used as a poultry market. You enter through the original bronze doors. Inside, the dome is a perfect semisphere, lit by a 9m oculus, a huge round hole, connecting the building with the heavens. If you're lucky enough to be around when the heavens open, you can watch the rainwater falling down in a column, draining away through holes in the marble floor.

Dedicated to all the gods, the name comes from the Greek words *pan* (all) and *theos* (god). General Marcus Agrippa built an earlier temple here in 27 BC and, although Hadrian constructed this version around AD 120, the façade's inscription reads 'Marcus Agrippa, son of Lucius, consul for the third time, built (it)'.

Consecration as a church in 606 helped save the building, though Pope Urban VIII still allowed Bernini to strip the ceiling's bronze cladding for reuse in St Peter's.

The first Italian king Victor Emmanuel II and the artist Raphael are buried here.

Stendhal wrote that he'd never met anyone who could remain impassive at this sublime sight. Another great thing about it, he added, is that you can visit it so quickly.

INFORMATION

☎ 06 6830 0230
✉ Piazza della Rotonda
€ admission free
🕑 8.30am-7.30pm Mon-Sat, 9am-6pm Sun
🚌 🚃 to Largo di Torre Argentina
♿ good
🍴 see p71

THE DOME WITH THE HOLE

Supported by structures within the concrete walls, the dome walls thin out from 5.9m to 1.5m at the top, and the concrete is also of gradually lighter density. Its diameter (43m) is equal to the building's height. The light-giving oculus also redistributes the building's huge structural forces.

THE SPANISH STEPS (4, G2)

Everyone hangs out on the Spanish Steps at some point. These broad, sweeping stairs lead down to elegant **Piazza di Spagna**, with Via Condotti running away as far as the eye can see. An ideal place to pose, meet and people watch, the steps resemble amphitheatre seating whose stage is the street.

Built in 1725 with French money (but designed by a Spaniard and named after the Spanish Embassy nearby) they were built to connect the piazza with the smart housing above. At the bottom of the steps, the **Barcaccia** (roughly 'the old tub') fountain is the last work of Pietro Bernini, father of better-known Gian Lorenzo. During the 18th century hopeful artists' models used to gather here in search of work.

INFORMATION

- ✉ Piazza di Spagna
- Ⓜ Spagna
- ♿ good (lift to the top from the metro)
- ✕ see p74

The area's been a magnet for foreigners since the 18th century, when so many Grand Tourists flocked here that it came to be known as the *ghetto de l'inglesi* (English ghetto). To the right as you face the steps is the house where romantic poet John Keats died in 1821, now a museum (p28).

Each April a fashion show is held in and around the piazza, and a blaze of pink azaleas floods the steps instead of chattering tourists.

ROMANTIC HOLIDAY HELL

In 19th-century Rome you could barely move for romantics. The consumptive Keats arrived in 1820, to improve his health. A three-week journey and 10-day quarantine did not help, and he died here in 1821 aged 25. Shelley drowned off the Tuscan coast. Byron at least survived his Roman holiday, writing *Childe Harold's Pilgrimage* ('Oh Rome! My Country! City of the Soul!').

Join the ranks of old-world Grand Tourists and loiter on the Spanish Steps

PIAZZA NAVONA (6, B2)

Huge, café-ringed Piazza Navona provides a spectacular baroque backdrop for everyday Roman life, simmering with excited kids, grumpy old men, critical caricaturists, pesky pickpockets and *gelati*-toting tourists.

Navona's centrepiece is Bernini's look-at-me **Fontana dei Quattro Fiumi** (1651) with the Nile, Ganges, Danube and Plate rivers representing the then-known four continents. Bitter rival Borromini was to be the fountain's architect, but Bernini won favour with Innocent X through his brilliant design and the canny present of a silver model to Innocent's sister-in-law. Facing the fountain is the **Sant'Agnese in Agone**, a church designed by Borromini. A favourite local yarn is that the Nile figure on Bernini's fountain is shielding his eyes to protect his gaze from Borromini's architecture. Boringly, the gesture indicates that the source of the river wasn't then known – the fountain was finished before Borromini had any involvement with the church.

Eclipsed by the central fountain, but continuing the watery theme, are 19th-century **Fontana del Nettuno** at the northern end (showing Neptune fighting a sea monster, surrounded by sea nymphs) and **Fontana del Moro** to the south, designed by Giacomo della Porta in 1576, with a central Moorish figure added by Bernini for reasons best known to himself.

INFORMATION

- ✉ Piazza Navona
- ⓘ Christmas market & funfair 1 Dec-6 Jan
- 🚌 to Corso del Rinascimento
- ♿ good
- ✖ see p71

Bernini's Fontana dei Quattro Fiumi

N'AGONA… NAVONA

This area housed Domitian's Circus Agonalis (corrupted to n'agona over time) and still preserves the arena's elongated shape. It hosted savoury sports such as jousting and racing – and less-savoury events such as the martyrdom of Sant'Agnese (see p36) – until the 15th century. It then became the city's main market for almost three centuries.

VIA APPIA ANTICA & THE CATACOMBS (3, E8)

Started in 312 BC, Appia Antica reached Brindisi (590km) in the south by 191 BC. It was the chief Roman route south, mentioned in the Bible, and nicknamed 'queen of roads'. Today it's still easy to see why. The cobbled road stretches out arrow-straight to the horizon, lined by cypress trees and ancient burial sites.

Ancient Rome banned burials within city walls, and the richest Romans began to establish roadside family mausoleums and build luxurious villas to show their status to passers-by. Early Christians also buried their dead out here, and lacking land, began to go subterranean. From the 1st to the 3rd centuries, they dug 300km of tunnels, filled with multistorey tombs. These were later damaged by barbarian invasions and abandoned.

There are three major catacombs to explore (on guided tours). **San Callisto**, largest and

Chiesa di Domine Quo Vadis on the Via Appia Antica

INFORMATION

- ☎ San Callisto 06 446 56 10; Visitor Centre 06 512 63 14
- ✉ Visitor Centre Via Appia Antica 42
- 🖳 www.parcoappiaantica.org; www.catacombe.roma.it
- € adult/concession €5/3
- ☺ catacombs 9am-noon & 2-5pm, San Callisto closed Wed & Feb, San Sebastiano closed Sun & Nov & Dec, Santa Domitilla closed Tue & Dec & Jan
- 🚌 bus 218 from San Giovanni, 660 from Arco di Travertino metro, Archeobus (hop-on & off €8)
- ✗ Cecilia Metella (p77)

most famous, once contained 16 popes and St Cecilia; fascinating **San Sebastiano** has a large basilica; and serene **Santa Domitilla** contains impressive frescoes and another big underground church.

On Sundays Via Appia closes to traffic and makes a fantastic excursion, on foot or by bike, starting at San Sebastiano and visiting the Catacombs, Circus Maxentius (p30), the Mausoleum of Cecilia Metella and Villa dei Quintili.

SAN SEBASTIANO ALUMNI

San Sebastiano is the only catacomb never forgotten and a continuous site of pilgrimage. An ancient inscription confirms that St Peter and St Paul's bodies were hidden here for 40 years. St Sebastian was also buried here (usually depicted covered in arrows, he recovered from this attempt on his life, but was subsequently executed).

PALATINE (4, H6)

Rome's most romantic ruins cover Palatine Hill, where everything started. This was where a she-wolf is said to have tended Remus and Romulus before Romulus killed his brother and founded Rome. Rome's earliest evidence of human habitation was discovered here: 9th-century-BC Iron Age huts.

As the most central of Rome's seven hills – and close to the Forum and attendant plebs – this hill was *the* residential quarter of the Republican and Imperial eras. Augustus was the first emperor to live here, relatively modestly in a private house, while Tiberius built the first imperial palace, followed and eclipsed by Nero and the Flavians. In the 16th century the area was converted into the **Orti Farnesiani** (Farnese Gardens).

A good place to start is **Museo Palatino** with decoration providing a sense of the sometime splendour of the *palazzi*. Most of the ruins are from Domitian's vast complex. Surrounding the museum are the **Domus Augustana** (meaning 'favoured by the gods', unrelated to Emperor Augustus), the private **Stadio di Domitian**, **Domus Flavia**, which covered the entire central plateau, the **Casa di Livia** (marvellous frescoes from here are preserved in Palazzo Massimo alle Terme, see p17) and **Casa dei Grifi**. Wonderful views sweep over Circus Maximus and beyond.

INFORMATION

- ☎ 06 3996 7700
- ✉ entrances at Via di San Gregorio 30 & Piazza di Santa Maria Nova 53
- € adult/concession €10/5 (includes Colosseum)
- ☽ 9am-1hr before dusk
- Ⓜ Colosseo
- ✗ take a picnic

A PROTECTIVE PALACE

Palazzo dei Flavi is distinguishable by a central octagonal brick maze. This courtyard was once lined with highly polished marble, that Emperor Domitian could use like a mirror to watch his back against assassination attempts. The tyrannical emperor was murdered, despite such precautions and his best efforts to kill off his enemies.

Play in the garden courtyard of Domus Augustana under the auspices of the gods

MUSEO NAZIONALE ETRUSCO DI VILLA GIULIA (3, C2)

Here lies Italy's finest collection of pre-Roman treasures, bilingually labelled and considerately presented in the 16th-century pleasure palace of Pope Julius III, with pretty frescoed loggias and a much-imitated *nymphaeum* (sunken pond).

The items, mostly from Etruscan burial tombs, show the extraordinary sophistication of this complex civilisation. The thousands of exhibits include beautifully engraved mirrors featuring expressive line drawings, gold jewellery, silver, extraordinary bronze figurines, huge bronze shields, counter games, black bucchero tableware (decorated with geometrical patterns and carved figures) and ancient imported items such as glassware from Assyria, Phoenicia and Cyprus. Enormous numbers of cooking implements show the Etruscan fondness for a good meal – Romans denigrated them for being fat.

Pride of the collection is the **Sarcofago degli Sposi**. This 6th-century-BC tomb for a husband and wife shows the almond-eyed happy couple reclining on its lid – a touchingly intimate portrait that shows an equality between the sexes rare in Republican Rome.

There is also a dazzling display of jewellery running from sophisticated 8th-century Etruscan items to contemporary pieces.

INFORMATION

☎ 06 322 6571, booking 06 82 46 20
✉ Piazzale di Villa Giulia 9
€ adult/concession €4/2
☼ 8.30am-7.30pm Tue-Sun
🚌 Via delle Belle Arti
🚊 Via Flaminia
Ⓜ Flaminio
♿ good
✖ museum café

Museo Nazionale Etrusco di Villa Giulia's fascinating frescoes

A PAPAL PLEASURE PALACE

Julius III's villa appears to be a noble country house, but on entering you realise that it's little more than a façade. The Roman aristocracy didn't live in such palaces, they were merely used for day or evening entertainments. Julius nevertheless spent fortunes on the house: 160 boatloads of classical statues were removed to the Vatican on his death.

TRASTEVERE (2, A2; 4, D6)

Trastevere means 'across the Tiber', and it's fitting that this beguiling quarter should be defined as elsewhere. It's the Roman Left Bank with its boho face, and has kept its medieval character – ivy-covered façades, labyrinthine lanes and graceful squares. After dark it's one of Rome's most happening districts, as people wander out for their nocturnal *passegiata* (stroll), filling the piazzas and cobbled lanes, and the busy restaurants and bars.

Romans from this area are Trasteverini, who consider themselves the true classical Roman descendants and quite distinct from other locals. Just to emphasise the point, in July they have a street party called *Noiantri* or 'we others'. However, this was an area for sailors in ancient times and its maritime connections attracted foreign residents right up to the middle ages. Trastevere still attracts overseas visitors who have come to live a Roman dream – there's even an American university in Via della Lungara.

The district centres on lovely Piazza Santa Maria, overlooked by its shimmering gold church (p35) mosaics and centred on a sparkling fountain restored by Carlo Fontana in 1692. Other attractions in the district include **Galleria Corsini** (p27) and hidden-away **Orto Botanico** (p42), **Villa Farnesina** (p39), **Santa Cecilia** (p34), **San Francesco a Ripa** (p33) and the **Tempietto di Bramante** (p39) with fabulous views from Gianicolo hill.

INFORMATION

- 🚋 to Viale di Trastevere
- 🚊 to Viale di Trastevere
- ♿ fair (cobbles)
- ✕ see p77

SANTA MARIA'S MOSAICS

Santa Maria's glittering 12th-century mosaics dominate Trastevere's central square. These show the Virgin flanked by 10 women bearing lamps (possibly wise and foolish virgins but the jury's still out). Two tiny kneeling figures were probably donors, and the bell tower bears another small mosaic of the Virgin. The portico, embedded with ancient and medieval fragments, was added by Carlo Fontana in 1702.

Piazza Santa Maria's fountain, restored by Carlo Fontana (wasn't he just born to do it?)

SAN GIOVANNI IN LATERANO (3, D5)

Fifteen figures surmount the façade of San Giovanni, as if ready to leap off. They're the finger-wagging apostles, John the Baptist and Evangelist, and Christ, a powerful rendering of the dominance of the church.

This is one of Rome's grandest churches, founded by Constantine. The papal headquarters until the 14th century, it's still Rome's cathedral.

Alessandro Galilei designed the 18th-century façade. Borromini transformed the interior a century earlier, creating a cool, classical space – the nave pillars are his, and trademark oval windows. Underfoot are marvellous 15th-century Cosmati mosaics.

Behind the first pillar on the right is a fragment of a Giotto fresco. While admiring it, listen out for the next pillar, where the Sylvester II monument is said to sweat and creak when the death of a pope is imminent.

INFORMATION

- ☎ 06 6988 6452
- ✉ Piazza San Giovanni in Laterano 4
- € admission free; cloister €2, baptistery €1; audioguide €5.50
- ⌚ basilica 8am-6pm; cloister 9am-6pm; baptistry 7am-12.30pm & 4-6pm
- 🚌 🚊 to Piazza San Giovanni in Laterano
- Ⓜ San Giovanni
- ♿ good
- ✗ see p77

A Gothic **baldacchino** towers above the papal altar. The huge, imposing **bronze doors** of the eastern façade are ancient Roman – from the Curia in the Forum.

Tread carefully – these mosaics have been here for half a millennium

The beautiful 13th-century **cloister** is an oasis of calm and delicately twisting columns. The baptistery, with some beautiful mosaics, was founded by Constantine but rebuilt in the 17th century.

Skip the long-winded audio tour, but do nip across to Scala Santa (p39) across the road.

CONSTANTINE & CHRISTIANITY

A general in the desolate outpost of England, Constantine was elected emperor by the army and soon converted to Christianity. Day-to-day, Christian values didn't appear paramount – he had his wife and son killed for plotting. But he did build San Giovanni's baptistery on his ex-wife's land. In 326 he shifted the capital to 'Constantinople' (today Istanbul).

GALLERIA DORIA PAMPHILJ (6, E2)

At Galleria Doria Pamphilj a magnificent private art collection is hung as it was in the 18th century. In the lavish, fusty apartments, paintings are used as a kind of wallpaper, with 400 works spread throughout the *palazzo* – the main gallery resembles a mini Versailles, with gold leaf, frescoed walls and mirrors. The audio tour provides an intimate insight into one of Rome's great families, with some great anecdotes.

The family heyday came during the papacy of family-member Innocent X, and their cosy relationship led to the word 'nepotism'. One of the collection's finest works is the Velásquez portrait of a canny-looking *Pope Innocent X,* who grumbled that the depiction was 'too real'. In the same room is Bernini's more distant bust of the same subject, a striking contrast.

Among the big names are Raphael, Tintoretto, Brueghel and Titian (including the powerful *Salome* holding the head of John the Baptist – apparently a self-portrait, with Salome modelled on his out-of-favour ex), as well as outstanding early works by Caravaggio, *Rest During the Flight into Egypt* and *Penitent Magdalen;* the artist used the same model for the Virgin and the prostitute.

The gallery of ancient Roman sculpture displays a fascinating jigsaw-puzzle of works, restored with new arms and heads.

As the audio tour picks out only a few highlights, it's easy to miss out other important pieces, so a catalogue comes in handy.

INFORMATION
- ☎ 06 679 7323
- 🖳 www.doriapamphilj.it
- ✉ Piazza del Collegio Romano 2
- € adult/concession €8/5.70 incl audio guide
- 🕒 10am-5pm Fri-Wed
- 🚌 to Piazza Venezia
- 🚹 good
- 🍴 café

DON'T MISS
- Macabre relic of St Teodora's body
- Guercino's *St Agnes*
- Brueghel the Elder's *Battle in the Bay of Naples*

More gilt than a row of confessionals in the Exhibition Hall in the Galleria Doria Pamphilj

Sights & Activities

MUSEUMS & GALLERIES

These cover the gamut from small evocative literary memorials to stunningly displayed excavations and galleries packed with great artworks.

Casa di Goethe (4, F1)
Johann Wolfgang von Goethe had a whale of a time in Rome from 1786 to 1788, and his flat is now a museum, with drawings and etchings by the great author as well as documents relating to his Italian sojourn and art inspired by him (including a Warhol portrait). He wrote part of his *Italian Journey* here.
☎ 06 326 50 412 🖳 www .casadigoethe.it ✉ Via del Corso 18 € €3/2 🕑 10am-6pm Tue-Sun 🚌 to Via del Corso Ⓜ Flaminio

Castel Sant'Angelo (4, C3)
Hadrian built the huge round building that dominates the river to serve as his mausoleum in the 2nd century. It was turned into a fortress in the 6th century – you can see the fortified passageway, built in 1277, connecting it to the Vatican. It contains some impressive Renaissance salons, and has memorable views, with a café on the ramparts.
☎ 06 681 91 11 ✉ Lungotevere Castello € €5/2.50 🕑 9am-7.30pm Tue-Sun 🚌 to Piazza Cavour

Centrale Montemartini (3, C6)
This is a truly extraordinary sight: ancient sculpture – Roman gods, goddesses, fauns and populace in gleaming marble (overflow from the Capitoline Museums) – displayed in an ex-power plant next to vast pieces of machinery. Well worth the slight trek.
☎ 06 574 80 30 ✉ Via Ostiense 106 € €4.20/2.60 🕑 9.30am-7pm Tue-Sun 🚌 to Via Ostiense Ⓜ Piramide 🚻 limited

Crypta Balbi (2, B1)
This excavated corner of the city hosts a scholarly, well laid out museum that shows the many layers of history beneath a city block – here Renaissance buildings lie above medieval merchant houses built over a Roman theatre. You also visit the foundations where you can see the historic strata.
☎ 06 399 67 700 ✉ Via delle Botteghe Oscure 31 € €9/6, ticket includes Palazzo Massimo Alle Terme, Palazzo Altemps & Terme di Diocleziano, valid three days 🕑 9am-7.45pm Tue-Sun 🚌 🚊 to Largo di Torre Argentina 🚻 fair

Galleria Colonna (4, G4)
This 17th-century gallery houses a splendid private art collection under loud, lovely ceilings painted by Sebastiano Ricci and others. The fabulous great hall is over 70m long and chandelier-, mirror- and cherub-packed. Tintoretto, Veronese, Salvator Rosa, Guido Reni and Guercino compete for your attention but it's Caracci's charming *Bean Eater* that catches the imagination.
☎ 06 678 43 50 🖳 www .galleriacolonna.it ✉ Via della Pilotta 17 € €7/5.50 🕑 9am-1pm Sat, closed Aug 🚌 to Piazza Venezia

Galleria Corsini (4, D5)
This graceful palace, once home to partying expat Queen of Sweden, has some wonderful *trompe-l'oeil* frescoes, and houses the other half of the National Art Collection (see also Palazzo Barberini, p28), including van Dyck's superb *Madonna della Paglia*, Murillo's *Madonna and Child*, Guido Reni's rich-hued *St Jerome* and melancholy *Salome*, and Giovanni Lanfranco's lovely *St Peter Healing St Agatha*.
☎ 06 688 02 323 🖳 www .galleriaborghese.it/corsini/ it/default.htm ✉ Via della Lungara 10 € €4/2 🕑 via 80-minute guided tour 9.30am, 11am & 12.30pm Tue-Fri, 8.30am-1.50pm Sat & Sun 🚌 🚊 to Viale di Trastevere 🚻 good

Rotund Castel Sant'Angelo

Galleria Nazionale d'Arte Antica – Palazzo Barberini (4, H3)

At splendid 17th-century Palazzo Barberini, you can compare Bernini's stately staircase with Borromini's breathtaking spiral version. Beneath a seething ceiling painting by Cortona, there are superb Caravaggios (including gloriously gruesome *Judith cutting off the head of Holofernes*), and more by Raphael, El Greco, Filippo Lippi, Tintoretto, Bronzino, Guido Reni and Hans Holbein.
☎ 06 481 45 91 🖳 www .galleriaborghese.it/barberini .it ✉ Via Barberini 18 € €5/2.50 🕓 8.30am–7.30pm Tue–Sun Ⓜ Barberini ♿ good

Galleria Nazionale d'Arte Moderna (3, C2)

This gracious *belle époque* palace houses an impressive array of 19th- and 20th-century greats, including Degas, Cézanne, Kandinsky, Mondriaan, Henry Moore and Cy Twombly. Among the Italians, there's Carrà, De Chirico, Lucio Fontana and Guttuso, the futurists (Boccioni, Balla) and the *Transavanguardia* (Clemente, Cucchi, Paladino). There's also a lovely café.
☎ 06 32 29 81 🖳 www .gnam.aribeniculturali .it/gnamco.htm ✉ Viale delle Belle Arti 131 € €9/7 🕓 8.30am–7.30pm Tue–Sun 🚌 to Viale delle Belle Arti 🚊 2, 3, 19 ♿ excellent

Galleria Spada (2, A1)

Highlight of this gallery is Borromini's clever 8m colonnade, which appears 35m long through the use of false perspective. The mannerist, stucco-studded *palazzo* is splendid, and contains the Spada family's former private collection, with works by Andrea del Sarto, Guido Reni, Guercino and Titian.
☎ 06 683 24 09 🖳 www .galleriaborghese.it/spada/ it/default.htm ✉ Piazza Capo di Ferro 13 € €5/2.50 🕓 8.30am–7.30pm Tue–Sun 🚌 116 to Piazza Farnese

Keats-Shelley House (4, G2)

Tragic Romantic poet John Keats spent his last few consumptive months here in 1821, and it's a moving sight to see the narrow room where he died, aged only 25. There are also letters home in spidery script, his life mask, and much more on him and other literary greats in Rome, including Shelley, Mary Shelley, Byron and Oscar Wilde.
☎ 06 678 42 35 🖳 www .keats-shelley-house.org ✉ Piazza di Spagna 26 € €3.50 🕓 9am–1pm & 3–6pm Mon–Fri, 11am–2pm & 3–6pm Sat Ⓜ Spagna

Museo Canonica (3, C3)

Sculptor and musician Pietro Canonica lived in delightful La Fortezzuola (the little fort) in Villa Borghese for almost 30 years before his death in 1959. There's a beautiful little orange tree–filled courtyard, and you can wander through the sculpture collection (mostly Canonica's own work), evocative private apartment and studio.
☎ 06 884 22 79 ✉ Viale Pietro Canonica 2 € €3/1.50 🕓 9am–7pm Tue–Sun 🚌 to Viale delle Belle Arti 🚊 19, 30

Museo d'Arte Ebraica (2, B1)

The only way to visit the city's splendid (and well-guarded) main synagogue (1904) is through admission to this tiny museum, which chronicles the fascinating historical, cultural and artistic heritage of Rome's Jewish community (Europe's oldest).
☎ 06 684 00 661 ✉ Lungotevere de' Cenci 15 € €7.50/3 🕓 10am–5pm Sun–Thu, 9am–2pm Fri Oct–Mar, 10am–7pm Sun–Thu, 9am–4pm Fri Apr–Sep 🚌 23, 63, 280, 780

Museo dell'Ara Pacis (4, E2)

Opened in April 2006, New York architect Richard Meier's beautiful Le Corbusier–influenced building seems more Big Apple than Eternal City. It looks like it's constructed from great pure-white Lego blocks, with two walls made entirely of glass, exposing the 1st-century BC

See the work of masters at Galleria Nazionale d'Arte Moderna

CONTEMPORARY CAPITAL

In recent years the Eternal City has begun to develop a contemporary edge. Some cutting-edge architecture is on its way – the first in a run of controversial new spaces is the Richard Meier–designed encasing for the Ara Pacis Augustae (opposite). The Zahia Hadid–designed, catchily named, Museo Nazionale delle Arti del XXI Secolo (MAXXI; 3, B2; ☎ 06 321 01 81; www.darc.beniculturali.it; Via Guido Reni 2), is a work-in-progress but houses temporary exhibitions, as does Odile Decq's Museo d'Arte Contemporanea Roma (MACRO; 3, D3; ☎ 06 671 070 400; www.macro.roma.museum; Via Reggio Emilia 54). MACRO and MAXXI are revolutionising the city's contemporary art scene and you can also see modern art in the classical Choistro del Bramante (see p34), or classical art in the modern Centrale Montemartini (p27).

'altar of peace', the museum's spectacular – and only – exhibit. Painstakingly pieced together by archaeologists, this is the first distinctive Roman sculptural work, and commemorates the victories of Augustus.

☎ 06 688 06 848 ⬜ www.arapacis.it ✉ Piazza Augusto Imperatore € €6.50/3 ☽ 9am-7pm Tue-Sun 🚌 to Piazza Augusto Imperatore

Museo Nazionale di Palazzo Venezia (6, E3)

Little-visited, this has some lovely gold-heavy Byzantine and early Renaissance paintings. The rest features porcelain, arms and bronzes, housed in the endless rooms of Rome's first great Renaissance palace, built for the cardinal who later became Pope Paul II. Mussolini's official residence, he made some famous speeches from its balcony.

☎ 06 679 88 65 ✉ Via del Plebiscito 118 € €4/2 ☽ 8.30am-7.30pm Tue-Sat 🚌 to Piazza Venezia ♿ good

Museo Nazionale Romano – Palazzo Altemps (4, E3)

This exquisite Renaissance palace has beautiful painted wooden ceilings and garden-frescoed loggias. The museum houses some of Rome's ancient treasure, splendidly lit; prize exhibits include the wonderful Art Deco–seeming 5th-century-BC Ludovisi Throne and the famous 6th-century *Galatian Suicide*. Many statues have been later 'improved', as was once fashionable.

☎ 06 399 67 700 ⬜ www.archeorm.arti.beniculturali.it ✉ Piazza Sant'Apollinare 46 € €7/3.50, or €9/6, ticket includes Palazzo Massimo Alle Terme, Crypta Balbi & Terme di Diocleziano, valid three days ☽ 9am-7.45pm Tue-Sun 🚌 to Corso del Rinascimento ♿ good

Palazzo delle Esposizioni (4, H4)

This vast 19th-century building, once Communist Party headquarters, was Rome's most prominent cultural centre, with a vibrant programme of multimedia events, art exhibitions, performances and cinemas. A 2004 roof collapse put an indefinite stop to reopening plans.

☎ 06 474 59 03 ⬜ www.palaexpo.it (Italian only) ✉ Via Nazionale 194 ☽ closed for renovation 🚌 to Via Nazionale ♿ good

Terme di Diocleziano (5, A3)

Across the piazza from Termini, Diocletian's baths (built at the turn of the 3rd century) were the largest in ancient Rome and could accommodate 3000 people. They are closed for renovation, but you can visit the beautiful 16th-century cloister designed by Michelangelo (for a convent built over the ruins), and the museum houses ancient epigraphs and artefacts.

☎ 06 399 67 700 ✉ Viale Enrico de Nicola 78 € €9/6, ticket includes Palazzo Massimo Alle Terme, Palazzo Altemps & Crypta Balbi, valid three days ☽ 9am-7.30pm Tue-Sun 🚌 to Termini Ⓜ Repubblica, Termini ♿ good

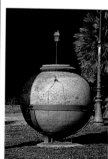

Ancient pot, gardens of Terme di Diocleziano

ANCIENT SITES & MONUMENTS

Rome is the world's finest open-air museum, with spectacular ancient sites popping up around every corner.

Arch of Constantine
(4, H6)

Built in AD 312 to commemorate Constantine's victory over his rival Maxentius, this magnificent triumphal arch is the best-preserved Roman memorial and one of the last built. As impressive as it looks, the arch is evidence of how Rome had by then fallen on hard times; the great sculptors' studios had closed and the arch was mostly made from parts pinched from older imperial monuments.

✉ Via di San Gregorio 🚌 Ⓜ Colosseo ♿ good

Area Sacra di Largo Argentina (6, C4)

The remains of these four Republic-era temples were revealed during construction work in the 1920s, close to the spot where Julius Caesar was slain. Surrounded by a busy bus and tram hub, it's now home to around 250 stray cats, and you can visit the ruins on tours organised by the volunteers at the cat sanctuary each Sunday.

🖥 www.romancats.de /romancats/index_eng.php ✉ Via di Torre Argentina € tours free 🕐 noon-6pm 🚌 🚊 Largo di Torre Argentina

Aurelian Wall (3)

The defensive wall built around the city by Aurelian in the 3rd century was shored up by medieval popes, and, incredibly, is still largely intact. It is almost 19km long, up to 10m high in places and once consisted of 383 towers and 18 gates providing access to the city.

🚌 118 to Porta San Sebastiano

Carcere Mamertino
(4, G5)

This is the Mamertine Prison, a dank dungeon for anyone who got on the wrong side of the ancient Roman authorities. Most famous internee was St Peter who was held here prior to his trial. Being Peter, he created a miraculous stream of water to baptise his fellow prisoners and dented

Colonna Antonina, a tribute to battles won

the wall with his head. The site is now the church of San Pietro in Carcere.

☎ 06 679 29 02 ✉ Clivio Argentario 1 € donation 🕐 9am-5pm 🚌 to Piazza Venezia

Circus Maxentius (3, E7)

Maxentius built this 3rd-century chariot racetrack for his private amusement (capacity 18,000). The starting stalls remain, along with ruins from the imperial residence (note embedded amphorae to lighten the walls). A Domitian obelisk from here was moved to Piazza Navona in 1650.

☎ 06 780 13 24 ✉ Via Appia Antica 153 € €3/1.50 🕐 9am-1pm Tue-Sun 🚌 see p21

Colonna Antonina (6, E1)

This 30m column, spiralled by vivid reliefs, was erected in AD 180 to commemorate Marcus Aurelius' victories in battle (against Germanic tribes at the bottom, and Sarmatians at the top). In 1589 Marcus was replaced on the top of the column with a bronze statue of St Paul.

✉ Piazza Colonna 🚌 to Via del Corso

More battles won, Colonna di Traiano

WHAT'S THE POINT?

While Mark Antony fell for Cleopatra, Romans swooned over Egyptian artefacts, and today 8 Egyptian obelisks puncture the Roman skyline (see Piazza del Popolo's version, right). The oldest and tallest of these is the obelisk in Piazza di San Giovanni, which was built for the Egyptian Pharaohs Thothmes III and Thothmes IV in the 15th century BC (3, D5; 42m). It was brought to Rome by Constantine in the 4th century and was placed in the Circo Maximo until it was buried by an earthquake in 1587. Unearthed in the 16th century, it was moved to San Giovanni by Pope Sixtus V, an obelisk fan.

Most-loveable-obelisk award goes to the 6th-century-BC needle surmounting a Bernini-designed elephant (6, D2; Piazza Santa Maria Sopra Minerva).

Colonna di Traiano (6, F3)
Trajan's column is decorated with superbly intricate reliefs – originally colourfully painted – depicting and celebrating victories over the Dacians (from modern-day Romania). It became Trajan's tomb, with his ashes underneath and a golden statue on top, later replaced by one of St Peter by Pope Sixtus V. Casts of the column at Museo della Civiltà Romana (p45) will save you much neck ache.
✉ Via dei Fori Imperiali
🚌 to Via dei Fori Imperiali

Domus Aurea (5, A5)
Nero's enormous and extravagant 'Golden House', con-
structed on land razed by the fire of AD 64, was built over by his successors and abandoned in the 6th century. The underground ruins were rediscovered in the late 15th century when Renaissance artists began studying the frescoed grottoes (which gave us the word 'grotesque'). The site has closed for long term works on the structure and to preserve the frescoes.
☎ 06 399 67 700 ✉ Viale della Domus Aurea
Ⓜ Colosseo ♿ good

Imperial Fora (4, G5)
The imperial fora of Trajan, Caesar, Nerva and Augustus were built between 42 BC
and AD 112. In 1933 Mussolini slammed through the highway from Piazza Venezia to the Colosseum, burying much of the remains, and their excavation is recent and ongoing. A visitor centre displays historical info and organises tours of the individual fora, most interesting of which is Trajan's.
✉ Via dei Fori Imperiali
€ tours €7 ☀ visitor centre 9am-7pm Tue-Sun Apr-Sep, 9am-6pm Oct-Mar
🚌 to Via dei Fori Imperiali

Mausoleo di Augusto (4, E2)
This unkempt shrub-covered mound was once one of ancient Rome's most imposing monuments, built in 28 BC as a mausoleum for Augustus and his descendants, and since been used as a fortress, vineyard and travertine supply. Mussolini had it restored, hoping to be buried here himself, and also put up the square's Fascist-era buildings.
✉ Piazza Augusto Imperatore € free 🚌 to Piazza Augusto Imperatore

Portico d'Ottavia (p32) – remants from 146 BC

OPERATIC LOCATIONS

Puccini's *Tosca* threw herself off the forbidding parapets of Castel Sant'Angelo (p27), and the church of Andrea della Valle (6, B3; Piazza di Sant'Andrea della Valle) and Farnese Palace (p39) also feature in the opera. Most-favoured dramatic settings are the Capitol and the Forum, with Samuel Barber's *Anthony & Cleopatra*, Wagner's *Rienzi* (which also features San Giovanni in Laterano, right), Mozart's *Lucio Silla* and *La Clemenza di Tito* and Handel's *Ezio* passing through. Berlioz's *Benvenuto Cellini* uses Piazza di Colonna and Arrigo Boito's *Nerrone* touches the Appian Way (p21).

Portico d'Ottavia (2, B1)

These few columns and a fragmented pediment that the neighbourhood has casually enveloped formed part of a 132m by 119m portico with 300 columns, enclosing temples, libraries and shops constructed in 146 BC and then rebuilt by Augustus in 23 BC. From the Middle Ages the portico formed part of the city's main fish market.
✉ Via del Portico d'Ottavia
🕙 lower part 9am-6pm
🚌 to Teatro di Marcello 🚃 8

Teatro di Marcello (2, B1)

An extraordinary sight: a Renaissance palace grafted onto a 1st-century-BC theatre (built by Augustus and used as a model for the Colosseum) by clever-clog architect Baldassarre Peruzzi.
✉ Via del Teatro di Marcello
🚌 to Teatro di Marcello 🚃 8

Tempio di Adriano (6, D1)

In a typically Roman merging of ancient and less-ancient, here 11 huge Corinthian columns dominate a small piazza, embedded into what was once the Roman stock exchange. They're all that remain of a 2nd-century temple dedicated to Hadrian.
✉ Piazza di Pietra 🚌 to Via del Corso

Terme di Caracalla (3, C5)

These 3rd-century baths could cater to 1600 punters, covered 10 hectares and included gymnasia, libraries, shops and gardens; below ground slaves sweated in 9.5km of tunnels, tending to the complex plumbing. Fragments of mosaic and statuary conjure images of the baths' former magnificence.
✉ Viale delle Terme di Caracalla 52 € €6/3 combined ticket with Mausoleum of Cecilia Metella & Villa dei Quintili 🕙 9am-1 hr before sunset Tue-Sun 🚌 628 to Via delle Terme di Caracalla
Ⓜ Circo Massimo

Trajan's Forum (4, G4)

The last, most ambitious of the imperial fora (AD 107-112), once measured 300m by 185m and comprised a huge basilica, libraries, the Colonna di Traiano and the elegant curved Mercato di Traiano, the Ancient Roman version of a multilevel shopping mall and office complex (partially closed during work on a new Roman Fora museum).
✉ Via dei Fori Imperiali
€ €5.10 🕙 9am-7pm Tue-Sun Apr-Sep, 9am-6pm Mar & Oct, 9am-5pm Nov-Feb
🚌 to Via dei Fori Imperiali

Teatro di Marcello – haven't I seen this somewhere before?

CHURCHES

As centre of the Christian world, Rome has a wealth of churches, with over 400 in the *centro storico* (historic city centre) alone, many containing incredible masterpieces. You could spend your entire visit doing the circuit – like many pilgrims before you – and hardly spend a cent (though take change for coin-operated lighting). They're a safe bet on Monday when many other sights close.

Il Gesù (6, E3)

Gold, gold, gold. Rome's first Jesuit church, built between 1568–1575, is the epitome of Counter Reformation architecture – worshippers were attracted to ecclesiastical activities by lavish doses of breathtaking splendour. Outstanding features are the 17th-century Il Baciccia ceiling fresco, with its tumbling figures, and the Andrea Pozzo altar.
☎ 06 69 70 01 ⊠ Piazza del Gesù € free ⊕ 6am-12.30pm & 4-7.15pm 🚌 to Piazza Venezia ♿ limited

San Carlo alle Quattro Fontane (4, H3)

Completed in 1641, this is one of Borromini's masterpieces: the elegantly curvaceous façade, interplaying interior convex/concave surfaces and the dome illuminated by hidden windows, all shoehorned into a tiny, awkward space. Borromini was so pleased with it that he asked to be buried here, but as he committed suicide, he was buried in an anonymous grave.
☎ 06 488 32 61 ⊠ Via del Quirinale 23 € free ⊕ 10am-1pm & 3-6pm Mon-Fri, 10am-1pm Sat, noon-1pm & 3-6pm Sun 🚌 to Piazza Barberini Ⓜ Barberini ♿ limited

San Francesco a Ripa (2, A3)

You can see here the rock St Francis of Assisi used as a pillow when he visited Rome, but this 17th-century church is most interesting for Bernini's is-she-or-isn't-she sculpture of the *Beata Ludovica Albertoni*, showing the nun having a sexually charged moment of religious ecstasy.
⊠ Piazza San Francesco d'Assisi 88 € free ⊕ 7am-1pm & 4-7.30pm Mon-Fri, 7am-noon & 4-7pm Sat & Sun 🚌 🚊 to Viale di Trastevere ♿ limited

San Luigi dei Francesi (6, C1)

Caravaggio's fantastically dramatic extravaganzas in light and shade, three canvases depicting the life of St Matthew, pull in the crowds to this French national church (Mass in French) although Domenichino's 17th-century frescoes featuring St Cecilia, second chapel on the right, are also worth a look.
⊠ Piazza San Luigi dei Francesi € free ⊕ 7.30am-12.30pm & 3.30-7pm Fri-Wed, 7.30am-12.30pm Thu 🚌 to Corso del Rinascimento ♿ limited

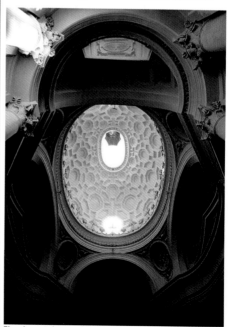
The elegant shapes of San Carlo alle Quattro Fontane

San Paolo Fuori le Mura
(3, B7)
This huge, echoingly empty church is the world's third biggest, and an imposing sight. Constantine built a basilica on the site of St Paul's burial in the 4th century, but it was destroyed by fire in the 19th century and later rebuilt. Fifth-century mosaics on the triumphal arch, a Romanesque paschal candlestick, Arnolfo di Cambio's 13th-century marble tabernacle and a beautiful Cosmati cloister – with twisting inlaid columns – survived. Beneath the altar lies St Paul's tomb.
☎ 06 541 03 41 ✉ Via Ostiense 186 € free
🕑 7.30am-6.30pm, cloister closed 1-3pm 🚇 Piazzale San Paolo Ⓜ San Paolo Ⓖ good

San Pietro in Vincoli
(4, J5)
Fifth-century San Pietro houses the chains that bound St Peter in the Carcere Mamertino (see p30), as well as Michelangelo's monumental, unfinished tomb of Pope Julius II. Some 40 figures were planned for the tomb but few were completed as Michelangelo got sidetracked by the Sistine Chapel and Julius didn't hang around to crack the whip (he is buried in St Peter's).
☎ 06 488 28 65 ✉ Piazza San Pietro in Vincoli 4a

San Luigi dei Francesi's (p33) dramatic ceiling

€ free 🕑 8am-12.30pm & 3-6pm 🚇 to Via Cavour Ⓜ Cavour Ⓖ limited

Santa Cecilia in Trastevere
(2, B3)
Here Saint Cecilia was (eventually) martyred in AD 230, after singing her way through various assassination attempts. When the patron saint of music's tomb was opened in 1599, the body was miraculously intact and sketched by Stefano Maderno for the exquisite sculpture beneath the altar. There are Roman ruins to visit below the 9th-century church, and precious fragments of a 13th-century Pietro Cavallini fresco.
☎ 06 589 92 89 ✉ Piazza di Santa Cecilia € free; crypt by donation 🕑 9am-1pm & 4-7.15pm Mon-Sat 🚇 🚊 to Viale di Trastevere

Santa Croce in Gerusalemme
(3, E5)
This pretty pilgrimage church was founded in AD 320 by St Helena, Constantine's mother, who went to Jerusalem and brought back Christian relics as souvenirs, including a piece of Christ's cross and St Thomas' doubting finger. (Constantine had hoped for a t-shirt but hid his disappointment.) The bell tower was added in 1144, the façade and oval vestibule in 1744.
☎ 06 701 47 69 ✉ Piazza di Santa Croce in Gerusalemme 12 € free 🕑 6.30am-12.30pm & 3.30-7.30pm Ⓜ San Giovanni Ⓖ limited

Santa Maria della Pace
(6, A1)
The outstanding feature of this church – besides Pietro

da Cortona's sinuous baroque façade and Raphael's *Four Sybils* fresco – is the beautiful 1504 Bramante cloister, now used for contemporary exhibitions (www.chiostro delbramante.it). Employing classical rules of proportion in this two-storey arcade, he managed to create a monumental feeling that belies its diminutive space.

☎ 06 688 09 036 ✉ Via della Pace € free, chiostro varies ⏱ 10am-12.45pm Tue-Fri 🚌 to Corso del Rinascimento ♿ limited

Santa Maria della Vittoria (4, J2)

This modest church is famous for Bernini's highly dramatic tableau, the *Ecstasy of St Teresa*, in the last chapel on the left. The saint is in rapture as a teasing angel pierces her repeatedly with a golden arrow. Whatever she's up to, it's a stunning, theatrical piece of baroque, bathed in soft natural light filtering through a concealed window.

☎ 06 482 61 90 ✉ Via XX Settembre 17 € free ⏱ 8.30am-noon & 3.30-6pm Mon-Sat, 3.30-6pm Sun Ⓜ Repubblica

Santa Maria della Vittoria

Santa Maria del Popolo (4, E1)

The first chapel was built on this spot in 1099 to exorcise the spirit of Nero, whose ashes were buried here. Transformed into this church in the 15th century, it's now a cornucopia of artistic treasures. Bramante designed the apse, Pinturicchio painted ceiling frescoes, Raphael decorated the Chigi Chapel and Caravaggio provided two spectacular paintings depicting the stories of SS Paul and Peter in the Cerasi Chapel.

☎ 06 361 08 36 ✉ Piazza del Popolo € free ⏱ 7am-noon & 4-7pm Mon-Sat, 8am-1.30pm & 4.30-7.30pm Sun Ⓜ Flaminio ♿ limited

Santa Maria in Aracoeli (2, C1)

Up a sweepingly dramatic 120 steps (local football hero Francesco Totti was married here), this simple 14th-century church has a surprisingly lavish interior that includes a 13th-century fresco by Cavallini, a beautiful, worn tomb by Donatello and frescoes by Pinturicchio. It's famed for the *Bambinello*, a wooden baby Jesus believed to have healing powers. The original was pinched in 1994 but the copy still apparently does the trick.

☎ 06 679 81 55 ✉ Piazza Santa Maria in Aracoeli € free ⏱ 9am-12.30pm & 2.30-5.30pm 🚌 to Piazza Venezia

Santa Maria in Cosmedin (2, C2)

Home to snappy sculpture the Bocca della Verità ('Mouth of Truth', see p43), this fine 8th-century church was built by merging an arcaded colonnade from a Roman market inspector's office with walls from a 7th-century Christian welfare centre. It was later enhanced with a 12th-century handsome seven-storey bell tower and portico. Inside is an Aladdin's cave for fans of Cosmati decoration.

☎ 06 678 14 19 ✉ Piazza della Bocca della Verità 18 € free ⏱ 9am-1pm & 2.30-6pm 🚌 to Via dei Cerchi ♿ good

Santa Maria in Trastevere (4, D6)

This beautiful church has wonderful 12th-century gold

mosaics on the Romanesque façade. Inside is a swirling Cosimato floor, more gloriously gold 12th-century altar mosaics, and fragments of exquisite 1st-century mosaic in the chapel left of the altar. You can leave notes for St Francis here too.

☎ 06 581 48 02 ⊠ Piazza Santa Maria in Trastevere € free ⏱ 9am-5.30pm Mon-Sat, 8-10.30am & noon-5.30pm Sun 🚌 to Viale di Trastevere

Santa Maria Maggiore (5, A4)

This is a fantastic barn of a basilica that includes a classical 5th-century triple nave, a Romanesque bell tower, kaleidoscopic Cosmati marble floor, a 15th-century gilded coffered ceiling, and fabulous 5th-century mosaics incorporated into an 18th-century façade. A marble slab to the right of the altar marks the tomb of Bernini, who was so instrumental in creating Rome's architecture.

☎ 06 48 31 95 ⊠ Piazza di Santa Maria Maggiore € free ⏱ 7am-7pm 🚌 to Via Corso Ⓜ Termini, Vittorio Emanuele ♿ good

Santa Maria Sopra Minerva (6, D2)

Rome's only Gothic church was built over the ancient temple of Minerva in the 13th century, then heavily restored in the 19th. It contains superb frescoes by Filippino Lippi (c 1489) in the Chapel of the Annunciation, Michelangelo's statue of *Christ Bearing the Cross* (gravity-defying bronze drapery was a later addition), and Fra Angelico's tomb.

☎ 06 679 39 26 ⊠ Piazza della Minerva 42 € free ⏱ 8.15am-7pm 🚌 to Corso Vittorio Emanuele II

Santa Prassede (5, A4)

Through an unassuming entrance, this wonderful church glows with jewel-like mosaics – Pope Paschal I had mosaic artists brought from Byzantium (later Constantinople) to decorate the church in the 9th century. The rich decoration covers triumphal arch, apse and almost the entire diminutive Cappella di San Zenone (which includes a piece of the column Christ was tied to when flagellated). Many ancient popes are buried here (having been

moved from the Catacombs).

☎ 06 488 24 56 ⊠ Via Santa Prassede 9a € free ⏱ 7am-noon & 4-6.30pm 🚌 to Via Merulana Ⓜ Cavour, Vittorio Emanuele ♿ good

Santa Pudenziana (5, A4)

Now a centre for Rome's Filippino community, this church has a magnificent 4th-century apse mosaic, the oldest of its kind in the city. An enthroned Christ is flanked by the apostles, although a barbaric 16th-century restoration chopped off two of them and amputated a few legs.

⊠ Via Urbana 160 € free ⏱ 8am-noon & 3-6pm Mon-Sat, 9am-noon & 3-6pm Sun 🚌 to Via Cavour Ⓜ Cavour

Santa Sabina (2,B3)

One of Rome's most beautiful churches, monumental and simple, this dates to 422 and is set on Aventine Hill. The original cypress-wood doors remain intact – featuring one of the oldest crucifixion scenes in existence. Twenty-four Corinthian columns separate the three naves, and are unusual in that they were made for the church, rather than plundered from ruins. There's a meditative 13th-century cloister.

☎ 06 579 41 🖥 ⊠ Piazza Pietro d'Illiria 1 € cloister €1 ⏱ 6.30am-12.45pm & 3.30-7pm 🚌 to Via del Circo Massimo ♿ good

Sant'Agnese in Agone (6, B2)

Borromini designed this cross-shaped church, built on the site of Sant'Agnese's

Santa Maria Maggiore has a little bit of everything

THE HOOLIGAN GENIUS

Caravaggio arrived in Rome aged 16 and proceeded to get in all sorts of trouble. If he wasn't having his commissions refused (an indecorous version of St Matthew and the Angel, Madonna with the Serpent for its crude realism), he was in other scrapes, as shown by contemporary police records: throwing stones at his landlady's windows, chucking artichokes at a waiter, and drawn-out quarrels over his girlfriend, a prostitute. Finally he killed a man in a duel and had to flee the city in 1606. He died four years later aged 37.

'The Inspiration of St Matthew' in San Luigi dei Francesi (p33)

martyrdom. Twelve-year-old Agnes refused to sleep with a Roman so was thrown naked in front of a jeering crowd. Hair grew to cover her nakedness and when soldiers tried to throw her on a fire, she didn't burn. Her impossibly small skull is proudly displayed in a chapel.
☒ Piazza Navona € free ☽ 9.30am-12.30pm & 4-7pm Mon-Sat, 10am-1pm & 4-8pm Sun ☐ to Corso del Rinascimento

Sant'Agostino (6, B1)

Works by Raphael and Caravaggio draw in the crowds to this 15th-century church. Raphael's fresco of Isaiah on the 3rd column in the nave, shows the influence of Michelangelo (both artists were working in the Vatican at the time), while Caravaggio's wonderfully natural *Madonna of the Pilgrims* is so stark that it was rejected by the commissioning church, who couldn't stomach the filthy pilgrims.
☎ 06 688 01 962 ☒ Via di Sant'Agostino € free ☽ 8am-noon & 4-7.30pm ☐ to Corso del Rinascimento

Sant'Andrea al Quirinale (4, H3)

Bernini designed this 17th-century theatrical chocolate-box of a church, with an elliptical floor plan and a series of chapels opening on to the central area. The interior is decorated with rose-coloured marble, stucco and gilding, and topped by cherubs flying around the dome lantern.
☎ 06 4890 3187 ☒ Via del Quirinale 29 € free ☽ 9am-noon & 4-7pm Mon-Fri, 9am-noon Sat ☐ to Via Nazionale ♿ limited

Santi Cosma e Damiano (4, H5)

Incorporating parts of Vespasian's forum, with a huge window onto the ancient structure, and dedicated to two doctors with miraculous healing powers, this church features a stunning, explosively coloured 6th-century mosaic depicting the Second Coming of Christ and a huge 18th-century Neapolitan *presepe* (nativity scene) off the cloister.
☎ 06 699 15 40 ☒ Largo Romolo e Remo € free, *presepe* donation €1 ☽ basilica 8am-1pm & 3-7pm; *presepe* 10am-1pm & 3-5.30pm Fri-Sun ☐ to Via dei Fori Imperiali Ⓜ Colosseo ♿ good

Santo Stefano Rotondo (3, D5)

Rome's remarkable first round church is ringed by antique granite and marble columns and decorated by Pomarancio's gruesome 16th horror-cycle of frescoes depicting various saintly martyrdoms, including beheading, impaling and – that old crowd pleaser – boiling in oil.
☎ 06 704 93 717 ☒ Via di Santo Stefano Rotondo 7 € free ☽ closed for restoration ☐ to Via Navicella ♿ limited

NOTABLE BUILDINGS & MONUMENTS

Home of so many aristocratic families and seat of religious and political power, Rome has a vast wealth of grand *palazzi* and structures.

Il Vittoriano – Rome's big friendly smile

Cimitero Acattolico per gli Stranieri (3, C6)

The non-Catholic cemetery for foreigners is the elegiac final resting place for numerous distinguished visitors who pegged it in Rome, among them Keats and Shelley. It's a moving, pretty spot, guarded by solemn-looking cats. Its pyramid stems from the ancient Roman craze for things Egyptian – it's a tomb built in 12 BC for Caius Cestius.
☎ 06 574 19 00 ⊠ Via Caio Cestio 6 € donation €2 ☿ 9am-5pm Mon-Sat Ⓜ Piramide

EUR (3, B9)

With a name sounding like an expression of disgust, EUR is nonetheless intriguing, a Kafkaesque complex of fascist architecture – including the blank-looking Palazzo della Civiltà del Lavoro: the 'Square Colosseum'. Mussolini constructed this ideal suburb for the Esposizione Universale di Roma, a 1942 international exhibition that never happened. It still feels faintly unreal.
⊠ EUR 🚌 160 Ⓜ EUR Magliana, EUR Palasport, EUR Fermi ♿ limited

Il Vittoriano (2, C1)

There's something endearingly horrible about this incredible monument in over-white marble commemorating Italy's first king, Vittorio Emanuele II. It's as graceful as an oversized set of false teeth, doing everything except jump up and down saying 'look at me' to get noticed, plonked beside the unfeasible grace of Michelangelo's piazza and the Forum. It's certainly handy for getting your bearings.
☎ 06 699 17 18 ☿ Piazza Venezia ☿ 9.30am-6pm Tue-Sun 🚌 to Piazza Venezia

Palazzo del Quirinale (4, G3)

This immense place was the Pope's summer pad for almost three centuries until, encouraged by a gun, he handed over the keys to Italy's new king (1870) and then the president of the Republic (1946). There's a free concert series at 11pm Sunday in the Maderno-designed chapel. The former stables house a magnificent exhibition space **Scuderie Papali al Quirinale**.
☎ 06 469 91 🖳 www .quirinale.it, www.scuderie quirinale.it ⊠ Piazza del Quirinale € *palazzo* €5.20 ☿ *palazzo* 8.30am-12.30pm Sun Sep-Jun; changing of the (two) guards 3.15pm Mon-Sat, 4pm Sun 🚌 to Via Nazionale ♿ good

Palazzo di Montecitorio (4, F3)

Built in 1653 by Bernini, this has been the parliament of Italy's lower house since 1871. It was expanded by Carlo Fontana in the late 17th century and given a larger façade by Art Nouveau architect Ernesto Basile in 1918. In 1998 Piazza di Montecitorio was restored to Bernini's original plan of a gently sloping ramp articulated by three radiating semicircles.
☎ 06 676 01 🖳 www .camera.it ⊠ Piazza di Montecitorio € free ☿ 10am-6pm, guided visits 1st Sun of the month 🚌 Via del Corso

Palazzo della Civiltà del Lavoro...err right

Palazzo Farnese (2, A1)

The French Embassy occupies this amazing palace, built in the 16th century under the successive supervision of three great architects, Antonio da Sangallo, Michelangelo and Giacomo della Porta. Inside are incredible frescoes by Annibale Caracci, only recently accessible to the public and visitable via guided tour (over 15s only). You'll need to book at least a few weeks in advance.

☎ 06 688 92 818 ⌨ visitefarnese@france-italia.it ✉ Piazza Farnese € free ⏱ 1hr free French/Italian guided tour at 3pm, 4pm & 5pm Mon & Thu 🚌 to Corso Vittorio Emanuele II

Ponte Fabricio (2, B2)

Rome's oldest intact bridge was built in 62 BC and connects the Ghetto and the Isola Tiberina (p41). It is known locally as 'the bridge of four heads' after its two busts of Janus, the two-headed God of doorways, passages and bridges.

🚌 to Lungotevere dei Pierleoni

Ponte Sant'Angelo (4, D3)

Built by Hadrian in the 2nd century as a route to his mausoleum, this is Rome's finest ancient bridge – the

Palazzo del Quirinale was the Pope's 'gift' to Italy's ruler

three central arches are original. In the 17th century, Bernini added the balustrade and 10 angels carrying the instruments of Christ's suffering, so the bridge became a symbolic passage for pilgrims to St Peter's. It was also a site for public executions.

🚌 to Piazza Cavour ♿ good

Scala Santa (3, D5)

These 28 wood-protected marble steps – said to be Pontius Pilate's staircase, scaled by Christ – are so holy that pilgrims climb them on their knees. In 1510, Martin Luther reached halfway before rethinking his religious priorities and heading back down.

☎ 06 704 94 619 ✉ Piazza San Giovanni in Laterano 14 ⏱ 6.15am-noon & 3.30-6.15pm winter, 6.15am-noon & 3.30-6.45pm summer Ⓜ San Giovanni

Tempietto di Bramante (4, C6)

Bramante's circular Tempietto fits its exquisite classical proportions snugly into the courtyard next to San Pietro in Montorio, built on a site thought to be the place of St Peter's crucifixion (St Peter's is considered the site of his martyrdom). Bernini added the staircase to the crypt and also contributed a chapel (second on the left) to the church.

☎ 06 581 39 40 ✉ Piazza San Pietro in Montorio 2 ⏱ church 8am-noon & 4-6pm, *tempietto* 10am-noon & 2-4pm 🚌 870 to Via del Gianicolo

Villa Farnesina (4, D5)

Raphael fans will delight in this charming villa containing masterly frescoes by the man himself including the *Triumph of Galatea*, and the *Cupid and Psyche* in the loggia. The villa was built in the early 16th century by the Sienese architect Baldassarre Peruzzi, who chipped in with a superb illusionary perspective of a colonnade and panorama of Rome.

☎ 06 680 27 268 ✉ Via della Lungara 230 € €5 ⏱ 9am-1pm Mon-Sat 🚌 to Piazza Sonnino

Book ahead for a chance to see inside Palazzo Farnese

PIAZZAS & PUBLIC SPACES

Rome's architects have an eye for dramatic open space and beautiful public works: piazzas and fountains are some of its most enchanting places.

Fontana del Tritone (4, H3)

In the middle of traffic-snarled Piazza Barberini, this was created by Bernini for his main patron, Pope Urban VIII, in 1642 (note the family crest). Four dolphins support a huge shell in which a strapping Triton, the sea God, sits blowing water through a conch.
✉ Piazza Barberini
Ⓜ Barberini

Fontana delle Tartarughe (2, B1)

This enchanting fountain shows four boys lifting turtles up into a bowl of water. Taddeo Landini apparently created it overnight in 1585, on behalf of the Duke of Mattei who had gambled his fortune away and was about to lose his fiancée (it worked, the Duke got the girl). Bernini added the turtles in 1658.
✉ Piazza Mattei
🚌 🚊 Largo di Torre Argentina

Fontana di Trevi (4, G3)

Setting of Anita Ekberg's *La Dolce Vita* romp, this epic fills an entire piazza. Completed by Nicola Salvi in 1762, out of the foam rears Neptune's chariot, with seahorses representing the sea's moods. Trevi refers to three roads *(tre vie)* that converged here. If you toss a coin in, it ensures

Toss a coin over your shoulder into the Fontana di Trevi

you a return visit to Rome.
✉ Piazza di Trevi 🚌 to Piazza di San Silvestro

Circus Maximus (3, C5)

Once some 200,000 spectators would gather to watch chariot races at Rome's largest stadium, decorated with statues and columns and used from the 4th century BC until AD 49. Now it's a neglected park, used mainly by joggers and dog walkers and for the occasional gig (such as Live8). It's best viewed from the Palatine hill.
✉ Via del Circo Massimo
🚌 🚊 to Viale Aventino
Ⓜ Circo Massimo

Isola Tiberina is the world's smallest inhabited island

Isola Tiberina (2, B2)
The world's smallest inhabited island is formed of volcanic rock. It has been associated with healing since the 3rd century BC, today home to the Fatebenefratelli hospital. There's also a cute, recently restored, 10th-century church and what remains of the *Ponte Rotto* (Broken Bridge), Rome's first stone bridge, is visible on the south side.

🚌 to Lungotevere dei Pierleoni

Piazza Campo de' Fiori (6, A4)
Vibrant Il Campo has a wonderful busy colourful market (selling fruit, veg, cheeses, meats) by day, while at night it turns into an open-air party, as the vaguely trashy cafés and bars overflow with local and foreign revellers. Towering over them all is Darth Vader lookalike Giordano Bruno, burned at the stake here for heresy in 1600. Bad loser Caravaggio went on the run after killing a man who beat him in a ball game here.

🚌 to Corso Vittorio Emanuele II 🚋 to Via Arenula 🚹 good

Piazza del Popolo (4, E1)
Northern visitors used to enter Rome via this magnificent piazza, a favoured spot for public executions. It was created in 1538 and given a neoclassical makeover in 1823. Carlo Rainaldi designed the (seemingly) twin 17th-century churches and Bernini did a number on the inner gate to celebrate Queen Christina of Sweden's defection to Catholicism.

Pick up your daily serve of fruit 'n' veg at Piazza Campo de' Fiori

The central obelisk hails from ancient Egyptian Heliopolis.

🚌 to Piazzale Flaminio 🚇 Flaminio 🚹 limited

Piazza della Repubblica (5, A3)
Laid out during Rome's 1870 makeover (when it became capital), this busy junction follows the line of the semicircular *exedra* (benched portico) of the ancient bath complex that stood here (see Terme di Diocleziano, p29). The nude frolicking of the nymphs in Mario Rutelli's *Fontana delle Naiadi* caused such a storm when unveiled in 1901 that the fountain

was promptly boarded up again.

🚌 to Piazza della Repubblica 🚇 Repubblica 🚹 limited

Piazza Farnese (2, A1)
Next door to Il Campo but a world away from its flurry and fruit'n'veg, this elegant piazza is dominated by the Palazzo Farnese (p39) and is most atmospheric in the evenings when the chandeliers of the palace are illuminated. The twin fountains' enormous granite baths came from the Terme di Caracalla (p32).

🚌 to Corso Vittorio Emanuele II 🚹 good

Piazza del Popolo is, happily, no longer an execution hotspot

PARKS & GARDENS

When you need a green escape, Rome has plenty. These wonderful inner-city gardens are just the place to recharge after cultural over-indulgence.

Orto Botanico (4, C5)

A perfectly positioned haven by Trastevere, these were formerly Palazzo Corsini's private grounds. The botanical garden has over 7000 species, including some of Europe's rarest plants, with stately palms, spiky cacti, dazzling orchids and more. There's a great hilltop view. ☎ 06 686 41 93 ✉ Largo Cristina di Suezia 24 € €4/2 ☼ 9am-6.30pm Mon-Sat (to 5.30pm Oct-Mar) ☒ to Lungotevere della Farnesina ♿ limited

Pincio (4, F1)

View collectors: don't miss this one – a superb sweep of the city with a brilliant bird's eye angle on Piazza del Popolo. Giuseppe Valadier designed the shady gardens

Get snap happy up at Pincio

(which adjoin Villa Borghese) in the early 19th century. ✉ access from Piazza del Popolo, Viale Trinità de' Monti or Villa Borghese ☼ 24hr ☒ to Piazzale Flaminio Ⓜ Flaminio ♿ good (from Viale Trinità de' Monti, lift from Spagna Metro to the Spanish Steps)

Roseto Comunale (2, C3)

The enchanting city rose garden has a backdrop of Circus Maximus and the Palatine. Roses bloom April to June and October. ☎ 06 574 6810 ✉ Via di Valle Murcia € free ☼ 8am-7pm Ⓜ Circo Massimo ♿ good (from Clivo dei Publici)

Vatican Gardens (4, A3)

It's well worth booking a tour to see the flower-filled French parterre, formal Italian garden and an English wood in the Vatican's backyard. The gardens feature fortifications, grottoes and fountains dating from the 9th century to the present day, tended by 30 gardeners. There's also a kitchen garden but you won't get close enough to press the papal tomatoes. ☎ 06 698 84 466 ✉ Città del Vaticano € €12/8 ☼ tours 10am Tue, Thu & Sat Mar-Oct, 10am Sat Nov-Feb ☒ to Piazza Risorgimento Ⓜ Ottaviano, Cipro-Musei Vaticani ♿ good

Villa Doria Pamphilj (3, A5)

Laid out by Alessandro Algardi in the mid-16th century, Rome's largest park, romantic and rolling, is ideal for a spot of recuperation beside a baroque fountain, feeding the ducks in the lake, or walking along picturesque walkways under parasol pines. A great place for kids. ✉ Via di San Pancrazio € free ☼ sunrise-sunset ☒ 710 to Via di San Pancrazio ♿ limited

Palm trees in Rome's Orto Botanico

ROMAN INDULGENCE

Rome can be an exhausting city: monuments to see, bumpy cobbles to walk on, traffic to avoid and shopping to do. To recuperate, spoil yourself.

Acanto Day Spa (6, C1)

A beautiful designer day spa, this is mosaic-mirrored, with stained glass, soft lighting and curvaceous white seating and a good place to go when you deserve a treat. They offer a wide range of massages and facials – a one-hour massage, facial or session in the large *hammam* (Turkish bathhouse) costs around €90.

☎ 06 681 36 602 ☐ www
.acantobenessere.it ✉ Piazza Rondanini 30 € €90
✆ 10am-10pm Tue-Sun
🚌 to Corso del Rinascimento

Cavalieri Hilton Hotel Pool (3, A2)

This gorgeous outdoor Olympic-sized pool is an oasis when the city sizzles, and has panoramic views too, perched on a hilltop. A sunlounger and a towel costs another €16, but you may as well splash out as you're here.

☎ 06 350 920 40 ☐ www
.cavalieri-hilton.it ✉ Via
Cadlolo 101 € €30
✆ 9am-7pm 🚌 991 to
Piazzale Medaglie D'Oro

Circolo del Golf di Roma (3, F7)

You need a handicap and evidence of an existing membership at a golf club at home to play at Italy's most prestigious golf club. It's a round like no other, through ancient ruins and with a Roman aqueduct. Weekends are usually members only.

☎ 06 780 34 07 ☐ www
.golfroma.it € €80 ✉ Via
Appia Nuova M Colli Albani

Hotel de Russie Spa (4, F1)

The spa at this marvellous palace hotel (see p97) is available to nonguests for €35, which allows you access to the Jacuzzi, sauna, treatment centre and gym. Treatments such as massage (Shiatsu, deep tissue etc) and facials start at around €90.

☎ 06 32 88 81 ☐ www
.roccofortehotels.com
€ from €35 ✆ 7am-9pm
(treatments 9am-
9pm) ✉ Via del Babuino 9
🚌 to Via del Corso
M Flaminio

Piscina delle Rose (3, B9)

There's notably more sunlounging than serious swimming going on at this attractive and huge open-air pool, surrounded by plenty of deckchairs, sunshades and people. You can be entertained by the aqua aerobics as you take it easy.

☎ 06 542 52 185 ✉ Viale
America 20 € €20
✆ 9am-7pm May-Sep
M EUR Palasport

Zodiaco (3, A2)

Zodiaco bar-restaurant is where Romans take their loved ones, the ultimate place for a sundowner high, high above the city. It's cheesily romantic but in a good way. Get here for sunset.

☎ 06 354 96 744 ☐ www
.zodiacoroma.it ✉ Viale del
Parco Mellini 88-90 ✆ 10am-
1am Mon-Thu & Sun, 10am-
3am Fri & Sat M Ottaviano

QUIRKY ROME

Here's a taste of Rome's eccentric hot spots – from rooms lined with bones to a surprising view through a hole in a door.

Bocca della Verità (2, C2)

Join the queue to put your hand in the drain. Legend says that if you put your right hand in the 'Mouth of Truth' while telling a lie, it will be bitten off (apparently priests used to put scorpions in there to help it along). In *Roman Holiday* Gregory Peck adlibs losing his hand and draws shrieks of unscripted terror from Audrey Hepburn.

✉ Piazza della Bocca della
Verità 18 € free ✆ 9am-
1pm & 2.30-6pm 🚌 to Via
dei Cerchi ⚭ good

Bocca della Verità – go on, test it out

Pasquino will tell it to you straight

Crypt of Santa Maria della Concezione (4, H2)

Mouth of Truth not quirky enough? Here lie the remains of 4000 Capuchin monks arranged in obsessive patterns. Spooky chapels contain blackly elaborate bone chandeliers, banks of skulls, and cloaked skeletons, some of which hold crosses and pray behind a sign that reads: 'what you are now we used to be, what we are now you will be'. Happy holidays! ☎ 06 487 11 85 ⊠ Via Vittorio Veneto 27 € donation appreciated ⏱ 9am-noon & 3-6pm Ⓜ Barberini

Museo Nazionale delle Paste Alimentari (4, G3)

Everything you wanted to know about pasta but were too afraid to ask: why is it better *al dente*? When was it invented? How is dried pasta created? And much more, from photos of pasta-munching stars, to a 13th-century will leaving macaroni as a bequest. ☎ 06 699 11 19 🖳 www .pastainmuseum.com

⊠ Piazza Scanderberg 117 € €9/6 ⏱ 9.30am-5.30pm 🚌 to Via del Tritone

Pasquino (6, A2)

This is Rome's most famous talking statue. During the 16th century, with no safe outlets for dissent, a tailor named Pasquino began sticking satirical verses lampooning the church and aristocracy here. Others joined in and pretty soon there were chattering statues all over town. You'll still see notices left here today. ⊠ Piazza di Pasquino 🚌 to Corso Vittorio Emanuele II ♿ good

Piazza dei Cavalieri di Malta (2, B4)

Up on Aventine hill is this peaceful little Cyprus tree–shaded square. It takes its name from the Knights of Malta, which has its priory here and an amazing secret viewed through the keyhole of its door – go and have a look. 🚌 to Via del Circo Massimo Ⓜ Circo Massimo ♿ limited (steep hills)

Sant'Ignazio di Loyola (6, E2)

Built to celebrate the canonisation of St Ignatius, the founder of the Jesuits, this church is full of fakes. The ceiling frescos pretend that the roof opens to the sky, faux columns line the church, and Jesuit artist Andrea del Pozzo created a convincing illusionary dome (stand on the yellow dot for the best view). ☎ 06 679 44 06 ⊠ Piazza di Sant'Ignazio ⏱ 7.30am-12.30pm & 3-7.15pm 🚌 to Via del Corso ♿ limited

ROME FOR CHILDREN

Italy has one of Europe's lowest birth rates, but not because Italians don't like children. *Bambini* (children) are feted and adored.

Pizza and ice cream is a child's dream diet and Romans are as good as dinosaurs – sights such as the Colosseum (p12), the creepy Catacombs (p21), and the Bocca della Verità (Mouth of Truth; p43) can all be hits. Villa Borghese (p13) is a fabulous place to go, with bike and pedal-car hire, pony rides, a boating lake and a tethered hot-air balloon.

Bellini Travel (p53) offers tailored tours and has some useful entertainment tips on its website.

Most sights are free for under-18s.

Bioparco (3, C2)

Going strong since 1911, this recently jazzed-up little zoo is a kid-pleaser if you've run out of other ideas. Concerted efforts are being made to

Funky elephant gate, Bioparco

make it more ecofriendly, with a focus on conservation and education. There are regular animal feeding sessions, and a farm, playground and little train.

☎ 06 36 08 211 🖳 www .bioparco.it ✉ Piazza San Pietro € €8.50/6.50 🕙 9.30am-6pm Mon-Fri, 9.30am-7pm Sat & Sun Apr-Sep, 9.30am-6pm Oct, 9.30am-5pm Nov-Mar) 🚌 217 to Bioparco 🚋 to Via Aldrovandi Ⓜ Flaminio ♿ limited

Let your child explore their inner adult at Explora

Explora – Museo dei Bambini di Roma (3, B3)
A fantastic museum that kids (up to 12) will love – hands-on, feet-on and full-on and a chance to play at the fun game of grown-ups – including at the post office, the hospital, the garage and the kitchen. It's brightly housed in the solar-powered wrought-iron-and-glass shell of a former tram depot. Great for rainy days and there's a good toy and bookshop.

☎ 06 361 37 76 🖳 www .mdbr.it ✉ Via Flaminia 82 € €6/free/7 adult/under 3/child 🕙 visits last for 1hr 45 mins & start 9.30am, 11.30am, 3pm & 5pm Tue-Fri; 10am, noon, 3pm & 5pm Sat-Sun 🚌 🚋 to Via Flaminia Ⓜ Flaminio

Gianicolo (4, B6)
The Gianicolo (Janiculum Hill) rises behind Trastevere and stretches to St Peter's. The views are fabulous although the kids might prefer the merry-go-round, pony rides, Teatro Pulcinella puppet show and the cannon fired at noon. ✉ Piazza Giuseppe Garibaldi € free (donation for puppet show) 🕙 puppet show various Mon-Fri, 10.30am-1pm Sat & Sun 🚌 870 to Via del Gianicolo ♿ good

Museo della Civiltà Romana (3, B9)
A giant model of 4th-century Rome brings it to life for kids and adults at this suburban museum, established by Mussolini in 1937 to glorify imperial Rome. There are detailed models, an absorbing cross-section of the Colosseum and casts of the amazing Colonna di Traiano (p31) reliefs.

☎ 06 592 61 35 ✉ Piazza G Agnelli 10, EUR € €6.20/3.10 🕙 9am-6.45pm Tue-Sat, 9am-1pm Sun 🚌 to Piazzale Agricoltura Ⓜ EUR Magliana ♿ limited

Time Elevator Roma (6, E2)
A 45-minute Hollywood-style romp through almost three millennia of Roman history, with much rousing music and many swirling togas. It uses panoramic screens and flight simulators, is a jolly good introduction to the city and, really, more fun than we'd care to admit. Another great rainy-day choice (over-fives only).

☎ 06 977 462 43 🖳 www .time-elevator.it ✉ Via Santissimi Apostoli 20 € €11/8 🕙 10.30am-7.30pm 🚌 to Piazza Venezia ♿ excellent (reserve & get 50% discount)

BABY-SITTING & CHILDCARE
Many of the larger hotels provide child-minding facilities and most others can arrange a sitter, but when in Rome you might prefer to do as the Romans do and just bring your kids along. If you want to find your own English-speaking babysitter, try **Angels Staff Services** (4, C2; ☎ 06 678 2877, mobile 0338 667 9718; Via dei Fienili 98; staffinitaly@yahoo.co.uk; per hr €14, per hr over 4 hrs €8, plus agency fee per day €20, per week up to 1 month €130).

Trips & Tours

WALKING TOURS

Introducing Rome

Facing **Il Vittoriano** (**1**; p38), veer right and take the *grander* steps up to Michelangelo's breathtakingly beautiful **Piazza del Campidoglio** (**2**; p14), flanked by the magnificent **Capitoline Museums** (**3**; p15). March beneath the right-hand medieval arch, hold your jaw to stop it scraping along the ground as the **Roman Forum** (**4**; p8) comes into view below. To ramble amid the ruins, return to the piazza and flop down Via di San Pietro in Carcere. Options on the way are **Santa Maria in Aracoeli** (**5**; p35) and the **Carcere Mamertino** (**6**; p30), where St Peter was imprisoned. On reaching

Ramble among the ruins of the Roman Forum

Via dei Fori Imperiali, you'll see **Colonna di Traiano** (**7**; p31) in front of the **Imperial Fora** (**8**; p31). Entrance to the Roman Forum is a little way up this road just to your right. After a wander take the main cobbled road, the Via Sacra, left to the **Colosseum** (**9**; p12). If you've anything left in the tank, take Via di San Giovanni in Laterano, on the far side of the Colosseum, and this will lead you to two outstanding ancient basilicas, **San Clemente** (**10**; p16) and **San Giovanni in Laterano** (**11**; p25).

Distance 3.5km (4km) **Duration** 2½hr
▶ **Start** 🚌 to Piazza Venezia ● **End** Ⓜ San Giovanni

A Stroll Through Centro Storico

After throwing a coin into **Fontana di Trevi** (**1**; p40), take Via de Crociferi and cross Via del Corso to **Colonna Antonina** (**2**; p30). Veer left along Via Canova Antonina, heading through narrow, pedestrianised streets. Turn left then right and follow Via dei Pastini until you reach the busy **Piazza della Rotonda** (**3**), from where the awe-inspiring **Pantheon** (**4**; p18) will introduce itself. Mosey along its left flank to Bernini's cute **Elefantino** (**5**; p31), then take Via della Palombella behind the Pantheon to Piazza Sant'Eustachio and have possibly the best coffee you'll ever have at the **café** (**6**; p72) of the same name. With a spring in your step, follow Via degli Staderari, jag a quick left on Corso del Rinascimento and then right into the brilliantly baroque **Piazza Navona** (**7**; p20). After completing a lap, take Via Pasquino to the piazza and **Pasquino** (**8**; p44), the mutilated 'talking statue'. Turn left and cross the busy Corso Vittorio Emanuele II to Via de' Baullari and the beating heart of modern Roman life, **Campo de' Fiori** (**9**; p41). What, no Renaissance? Take any of the narrow streets on the far side of Il Campo – will Michelangelo's **Palazzo Farnese** (**10**; p39) suffice?

Fontana di Trevi and Neptune's rearing chariot never fail to impress

Distance 2.5km **Duration** 1½hr ▶ **Start** 🚌 to Piazza San Silvestro, Ⓜ Barberini ● **End** 🚌 from Corso Vittorio Emanuele II

Amble Through Villa Borghese

For a break from crowds and carbon monoxide, climb (or take the lift just inside Spagna Metro) up the **Spanish Steps** (1; p19) and take a right along Via Sistina and left into Via di Porta Pinciana. You'll skirt the **Aurelian Wall** (2; p30) to your left, before entering **Villa Borghese** (3; p13). Go right along Viale del Museo Borghese to reach stunning **Galleria Borghese** (4; p13). A left here will bring you to **Bioparco** (5; p44). Cross-country down a small track, up through a dip, and **Museo Canonica** (6; p28) appears on your right. **Piazza di Sienna** (7; p95), an 18th-century amphitheatre used for equestrian events, is on your left. Carry on along Viale Pietro Canonica and when you see the **Tempio di Esculapio** (8) in the distance to your right, follow it to a pretty lake. Recharged and ready for Rome, return to the main thoroughfare and carry on through Viale delle Magnolie until you reach the **Pincio** (9; p42) with breathtaking views of St Peter's Basilica and **Piazza del Popolo** (10; p41). Descend the steps for refreshments in either of the two historic cafés below. Follow your political instincts; left to Rosati or right to Canova.

Distance 4km **Duration** 3hr
▶ **Start** Ⓜ Spagna
● **End** Ⓜ Flaminio

The Spanish Steps is a great spot for some people-watching

Piazza Farnese to St Peter's

In **Piazza Farnese** (**1**; p41), facing **Palazzo Farnese** (**2**; p39), take the road left of the palace and follow it to the end. Then turn right onto **Via Giulia** (**3**), noting **Fontana del Mascherone** (**4**), a baroque fountain combining an ancient grotesque mask and stone basin. Just beyond it Michelangelo's **Arco Farnese** (**5**) drips with ivy. Two giant falcon heads mark the **Palazzo Falconieri** (**6**; Via Giulia 1).

Continue on Via Giulia and to the left, in Via di Sant'Eligio, is **Chiesa di Sant'Eligio degli Orefici** (**7**), the 16th-century, Raphael-designed goldsmiths' church. Amble along and to your right is **Palazzo Ricci** (**8**), famous for the façade's 16th-century frescoes. Further along on the left are the **Carceri Nuove** (**9**, New Prisons), built in 1655 and used as a prison until the 19th century. There are several elaborate **Renaissance palaces** (**10**) at Via Giulia's northern end, an area sometimes known as the Quartiere Fiorentino after a sometime Florentine colony.

At the end of Via Giulia, turn right and follow the Tiber as far as dramatic **Ponte Sant'Angelo** (**11**; p39). Cross the river to **Castel Sant'Angelo** (**12**; p27), then follow the 13th-century papal escape route, the **passetto** (**13**), along Borgo Sant'Angelo to **St Peter's Square** (**14**; p9).

Hadrian's heavily fortified Castel Sant'Angelo

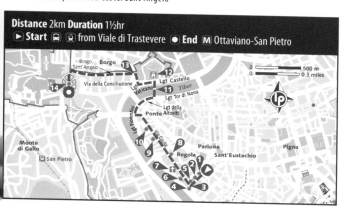

Distance 2km **Duration** 1½hr
▶ **Start** 🚌 🚊 from Viale di Trastevere ● **End** Ⓜ Ottaviano-San Pietro

DAY TRIPS
Ostia Antica (1, A2)

A 4th-century BC port (ostium means 'river mouth'), Ostia Antica's ruins are an amazing insight into everyday ancient-Roman life. You can wander around a café so intact that the menu still hangs over the bar, visit a tavern, and wonder at communal toilets.

Rome's main port for six centuries (populated by merchants, sailors and slaves), the city was abandoned after Barbarian invasions. Fortunately for us, it became buried in silt, and hence the remains rival Pompeii in their completeness.

The 1km-long main thoroughfare, **Decumanus Maximus**, connects the Porta Romana and the Porta Marina, entrances to the city and sea (the river changed its course after a 1557 flood, leaving the port landlocked).

Behind the restored **theatre** is the **Piazzale delle Corporazioni**, Ostia's merchant guild offices, with mosaics depicting different trades. Second-century **Casa di Diana** is a pristine example of ancient high-density housing. Nearby is the remarkable **Thermopolium**, an ancient café, complete with frescoed menu.

At the Forum Baths, you can see an intact roomful of absurdly fascinating **forica** – ancient toilets. Further along is the meat market, with a fish mosaic advertising the fishmonger's stand. At **Caupona di Alexander Helix**, a small inn, floor mosaics show popular athletes of the day.

Allow several hours to wander. It's worth buying a plan (€2). Don't miss the superb **Museo Ostiense**, displaying statuary and sarcophagi discovered here, including stunning Mithraic pieces.

INFORMATION
25km southwest of Rome

- Ⓜ Piramide, then Lido train to Ostia Antica (25min)
- ☎ 06 563 52 830
- ✉ Viale dei Romagnoli 717, Ostia Antica
- € adult/child €4/2, audio guide €4
- ☙ 9am-7pm Tue-Sun Apr-Oct, 9am-5pm Nov-Feb, 9am-6pm Mar (last admission 1hr before close)
- ✖ restaurant/café (but bring a picnic)

The Roman theatre with 2400 years of jaffas rolling down its aisles

Tivoli (1, C1)

Hilltop Tivoli, above the Aniene River, has been a popular summer retreat for prominent Romans since their army conquered it in 4th century BC. Here lie the ruins of Imperial Rome's most sumptuous pad, Hadrian's 2nd-century **Villa Adriana** (Via di Villa Adriana; adult/child €6.50/3.25; 9am-1½hr before sunset), today a Unesco World Heritage site.

Wouldn't you love to see anything performed here at picturesque Teatro Marittimo?

It's more like a city than a house, a rambling complex of barracks, nymphaeums, temples and water features. A model near the entrance supplies an idea of the scale. The well-travelled emperor designed parts of the vast complex himself, and sections are inspired by buildings in Greece and Egypt. Highlights include the fishpond with an underground walkway, and the emperor's private retreat, the **Teatro Marittimo**, on an artificial island accessed only by a retractable wooden bridge (replaced by a concrete version) and surrounded by colonnades.

Nearby, **Villa d'Este** (Piazza Trento; adult/child €6.50/3.25; 8.30am-6.30pm Tue-Sun Apr-Sep, 8.30am-4.30pm Oct-Mar) is another extravagant pleasure palace, this time built for Cardinal Ercole d'Este during the devil-may-care extravagance of the 16th century. The building is prettily frescoed, but it's the stunning formal gardens with their 51 complex fountains (including ones that played tunes and imitate bird calls) that are the real stars of the show.

INFORMATION

31km northeast of Rome

- Ⓜ Rebibbia, then Cotral bus (30min) to Largo Garibaldi, walk to Villa d'Este, bus 4 to Villa Adriana
- 🚗 take the A24 from Rome
- ℹ tourist office (☎ 0774 311 249), Largo Garibaldi
- ✗ restaurants, but bring a picnic

Cerveteri (1, A1)

Here is a town of tombs. Etruscan Cerveteri was one of the most powerful commercial centres in the Mediterranean from 7th to 5th century BC. All that remains is the ancient **Banditaccia Necropolis** (☎ 06 994 00 01; admission €4; 🕙 9am-4pm Tue-Sun Sep-May, 9am-7pm Tue-Sun Jun-Aug). Mounds of earth with carved stone bases are laid out as a town, with streets, squares and rows of tomb-houses. The best example is 4th-century-BC **Tomba dei Rilievi**, with painted reliefs of household items. Treasures from the tombs can be seen at the **Museo Nazionale di Cerveteri** (☎ 06 994 13 54; admission €4; 🕙 9am-7pm Tue-Sun) in the town centre, and in the Vatican Museums (p10) and Villa Giulia (p23).

INFORMATION
45km northwest of Rome
- 🚌 from Lepanto (1hr 10min), hourly shuttles to tombs (2km)
- ℹ️ tourist office (☎ 06 995 52 637, Piazza Risorgimento 19)
- 🍴 Antica Locanda Le Ginestre, Piazza Santa Maria 5

Beautiful relief sculptures on an Etruscan tomb, Cerveteri

Castelli Romani (1, C2)

In the green Colli Albani (Alban Hills), 'Roman Castles' are small towns thus called because wealthy Romans used to build their summer *palazzi* here.

Frascati (321m) offers stunning views. Dominating the small town is Villa Aldobrandini, a magnificent 16th-century mansion – to visit get a permit from the tourist office. One of the best things you can do is head into the backstreets for some Frascati wine and *porchetta* (roast ham with herbs) and traditional biscuits dipped into your wine as dessert.

Castelgandolfo is the Pope's summer address, a charming hilltop *borgo* overlooking beautiful volcanic **Lago di Albano**, where it's possible to swim or go boating.

INFORMATION
20km southeast of Rome
- 🚌 from Anagnina
- 🚆 Frascati/Castel Gandolfo from Termini 30/40min
- ℹ️ Frascati Tourist Office (☎ 06 942 03 31; Piazza G Marconi)
- 🍴 restaurants

ORGANISED TOURS

Archeobus
A fabulous tour along the Appia Antica that includes the catacombs and 2nd-century Villa dei Qinitili (the largest estate outside Rome). The air-conditioned 15-seater bus is hop-on/off.
☎ 06 469 54 695 € €7.75 buy on board ☼ buses depart Piazza Venezia every hr 10am-5pm

Battelli di Roma (4, D3)
Riverboats depart Ponte Sant'Angelo and make a 70-minute circuit via Isola Tiberina. There's an Ostia Antica trip (2½ hours) from Ponte Marconi too. You can use the boat as transport (€1; Stadio Flaminio–Isola Tiberina).
☎ 06 678 93 61 ☐ www.battellidiroma.it ✉ Ponte Sant'Angelo € €12 ☼ varies

Bellini Travel
This UK agency offers some great tours for kids, such as the Fountain or the San Clemente time machine tour, as well as walks for grownups, on themes such as mosaics.
☎ +44 20 7602 7602 ☐ www.bellinitravel.com ✉ 7 Barb Mews, London, W6 7PA € per 2hr/full day £150/300 ☼ varies

Ciao Roma
This small hop-on/off bus – resembling an old trolley car – stops at many of the city's best attractions and has entertaining, informative commentary in many languages (on tape with earphones).
☎ 06 489 76 161 € €18, no hop off €12, with

'Hey look, isn't that Russell Crowe?' – the Colosseum

Borghese Gallery entrance €24 ☼ 8.30am-6pm

Context Rome
Context Rome offers thematic tours and tailor-made itineraries led by scholars specialising in art history, architecture and archaeology. Tours include Renaissance Rome, Jewish Ghetto and Trastevere, and the Sistine Chapel. They also run high-season trips to sights usually closed to the public.
☎ 06 482 09 11 ☐ www.scalareale.org ✉ Via Baccina 40 € per person €25-150 ☼ varies

Enjoy Rome (5, B3)
Pitched at young, independent travellers, Enjoy Rome offers themed three hour walking tours in groups of maximum 25. There's a more expensive trip to the catacombs and the Appian Way.
☎ 06 445 68 90 ☐ www.enjoyrome.com ✉ Via Marghera 8a € €24-40,

under 26 €15-30 ☼ office 8.30am-7pm Mon-Fri, 8.30am-2pm Sat

Through Eternity Rome
Enthusiastic, animated storytellers make Rome come alive, offering a range of tours from twilight Rome to the 'Feast of Bacchus' wine sampler. You can also discover Rome on treasure hunts or private tours.
☎ 06 700 93 36 ☐ www.througheternity.com € €20-50 ☼ varies

Vastours
Vastours offer diverse themed tours, including Ancient, Christian, Monumental and Artistic Rome as well as Papal audiences; also offers trips to Ostia Antica and Tivoli.
☎ 06 481 43 09 ☐ vastours@vastours.it ✉ Via Piemonte 34 € Rome tours, including admission charges, €32.50-72, Tivoli or Ostia €49 ☼ varies

Shopping

Not only is Rome astonishingly beautiful and packed with ancient history and beautiful masterpieces, but it's a great place to shop. One of the charms is that chain stores haven't taken much hold here, so the streets are filled with one-off boutiques that you won't find anywhere else. Italy also still takes pride in its manufacturing, being a producer of superb-quality shoes, clothes, leather goods, furniture and design, as well as, of course, food and wine. Whether you are window shopping or flexing the plastic, Rome's boutiques exert a beguiling pull – you may have to invest in some more luggage.

Shopping Areas

Spreading from the **Spanish Steps** (4, G2) is a grid of narrow cobbled streets, including Via Condotti, Via Frattina and Via Borgognona, loaded with fashion's big guns (Dolce & Gabbana, Prada, Versace, etc) and small high-end boutiques, with shops like temples to clothes. **Via del Corso** (4, F2) is a big shopping drag (lots of street wear and high-street shops), with trashy and classy places rubbing shoulders, while **Via Nazionale** (4, H4) and **Via dei Giubbonari** (2, A5) are also both full of upper-end, high-street clothing. For vintage, and upcoming Roman designers, check out **Via del Governo Vecchio** (6, A2), a wonderful street lined with treasure-trove boutiques. Across the river, near the Vatican, **Via Cola di Rienzo** (4, C2) has a good selec-

Buy your very own masterpiece at Piazza Navona

tion of clothing, shoes and food shops while the narrow medieval streets of Trastevere and around Campo de' Fiori, such as Via del Pellegrino, are home to lots of interesting little boutiques, gift and design shops, workshops and studios.

Rome's markets are a great place for hunting down bargains and gifts. The best known is Trastevere's huge, trashy **Porta Portese** (p62), although there are several smaller, specialised markets worth a visit (p62). If you're looking for high-end antiques, art, design or unusual souvenirs, try **Via Giulia** (4, D4), **Via dei Coronari** (6, A1), **Via Margutta** or **Via del Babuino** (4, F1).

OPENING HOURS

Shops usually open from 9.30am to 1pm and from 3.30pm to 7.30pm (winter) or 4pm to 8pm (summer), although small boutiques might open later and close earlier. There is a trend, particularly on main tourist thoroughfares and among larger shops and department stores, to stay open throughout the day.

FASHION

As well as all fashion's big names, here are myriad small independent boutiques with original pieces — perfect for discovering beautiful clothes that you're unlikely to spot on someone else. Also bear in mind several top designers have diffusion ranges aimed at younger tastes and (marginally) slimmer budgets, all with stores around the Spanish Steps.

Alberta Ferretti (4, F2)

Delicate, cobweb-fine, deliciously beautiful clothes are the hallmark of Alberta Ferretti. 'Philosophy' is an amazing diffusion line under her main collection, renowned for fine spaghetti strap dresses and a strong 1920s and '30s influence. She also does original shoes. ☎ 06 679 77 28 ⊠ Via Condotti 34 🕒 10am-7.30pm Mon-Sat Ⓜ Spagna

Angelo di Nepi (4, B2)

This Roman designer's jewel-like boutique sells original, exquisitely made coats, skirts, trousers, tops and scarves, using bright colours and beautiful Indian fabrics. There are other branches at Via Frattina 2 and Via dei Giubbonari. ☎ 06 322 48 00 ⊠ Via Cola di Rienzo 267a 🕒 12.30-7.30pm Mon, 9.30am-7.30pm Tue-Sat 🚌 to Piazza del Risorgimento Ⓜ Ottaviano

Baullà (6, A4)

This gem of a shop between Campo de' Fiori and Piazza Farnese sells excellent-quality, ethnic-flavoured knits, original coats and jackets, skirts, tops, bags, scarves and accessories. ☎ 06 686 76 70 ⊠ Via de' Baullari 37 🕒 4-7.30pm Mon, 10am-7.30pm Tue-Sat 🚌 Corso Vittorio Emanuele II

Brighenti (4, G2)

You can imagine Sophia Loren popping in here for a well-structured something. Luxurious lingerie and too-good-to-get-wet swimming costumes for the stars are the speciality of wonderfully old-fashioned Brighenti with lots of frothy displays under voluminous chandeliers. ☎ 06 679 14 84 ⊠ Via Frattina 7-10 🕒 3.30-7.30pm Mon, 10am-2pm & 3.30-7.30pm Tue-Thu, 10am-7.30pm Fri & Sat Ⓜ Spagna

Cenci (4, E3)

This famous Roman institution near the Pantheon stocks a big selection of top Italian and international labels for men, women and children. Expect beautifully cut, classic fashions on the conservative side of English country squire. ☎ 06 699 06 81 ⊠ Via di Campo Marzio 1/7 🕒 3.30-7.30pm Mon, 9.30am-1.30pm & 3.30-7.30pm Tue-Fri, 10am-7.30pm Sat 🚌 to Via del Corso

Diesel (4, F2)

Diesel, purveyor of low slung jeans and inventive, clubby

Purchase some exceptionally engineered undies at Brighenti

clothes, is an Italian brand, and its Roman flagship store has a good selection of what makes the hoards keep coming back. There's a second shop at Via del Babuino 94 (☎ 06 693 80 053).
☎ 06 678 39 33 ⊠ Via del Corso 186 ⌚ 10.30am-7.30pm Mon-Sat, 3-7.30pm Sun 🚌 to Via del Corso

Dolce e Gabbana (4, F2)
Rock-star edge, cheeky styling and unapologetic sexuality are the signatures of this famous Italian designer duo who dress A-list celebrities (and beautifully clothed nonentities) all over the world. Clothes to make a statement and be centre of attention.
☎ 06 679 22 94 ⊠ Piazza di Spagna 94-95 ⌚ 1-7.30pm Mon, 10am-7.30pm Tue-Sat, 11am-7.30pm Sun Ⓜ Spagna

Ethic (2, A1)
Eclectic, boho, vintage-style, but thoroughly modern womenswear in interesting fabrics from this affordable, original Italian chain includes clothes,

bags, accessories and shoes. There are further branches at Via del Corso 85 (☎ 06 360 02 191) and Via del Pantheon 50 (☎ 06 688 03 167).
☎ 06 6830 10 63 ⊠ Piazza Cairoli 11 ⌚ 10am-8pm Tue-Sat, noon-8pm Sun & Mon 🚋 Via Arenula

Fendi (4, F2)
No self-respecting *fashionista* will be seen unarmed with a Fendi baguette – their bags set the seasonal standard. This vast store also sells deeply glamorous furniture to recline on in your natty threads. There's another huge branch on Via del Corso.
☎ 06 69 66 61 ⊠ Via Borgognona 36 ⌚ 10am-7.30pm Mon-Sat, 11am-2pm & 3pm-7pm Sun Ⓜ Spagna

Gianni Versace (4, F2)
You too can look like Donatella Versace. If you've got a premiere where you want to strike a dash, or want some superbly high-end, high-camp trashy fashion, head here and glitz it up.
☎ 06 678 05 21 ⊠ Via Bocca di Leone 26 ⌚ 10am-

7pm Mon-Sat, 2-7pm Sun Ⓜ Spagna

Giorgio Armani (4, F2)
Giorgio Armani's clothes are subtle, exceptionally cut, using considered palettes and gorgeous fabrics. Here you'll find his range of elegant ready-to-wear suits and separates for men and women: clothes for celebrities making an understated statement.
☎ 06 360 02 197 ⊠ Via Condotti 76 ⌚ 3.30-7.30pm Mon, 10am-7.30pm Tue-Sat Ⓜ Spagna

Gucci (4, F2)
Barely needing any introduction, and most beloved of fake-bag sellers around town, is Gucci. Fabulous shoes, bags and sexy little

CLOTHING & SHOE SIZES

Women's Clothing

Aust/UK	8	10	12	14	16	18
Europe	36	38	40	42	44	46
Japan	5	7	9	11	13	15
USA	6	8	10	12	14	16

Women's Shoes

Aust/USA	5	6	7	8	9	10
Europe	35	36	37	38	39	40
France only	35	36	38	39	40	42
Japan	22	23	24	25	26	27
UK	3½	4½	5½	6½	7½	8½

Men's Clothing

Aust	92	96	100	104	108	112
Europe	46	48	50	52	54	56
Japan	S	M	M		L	
UK/USA	35	36	37	38	39	40

Men's Shirts (Collar Sizes)

Aust/Japan	38	39	40	41	42	43
Europe	38	39	40	41	42	43
UK/USA	15	15½	16	16½	17	17½

Men's Shoes

Aust/UK	7	8	9	10	11	12
Europe	41	42	43	44½	46	47
Japan	26	27	27.5	28	29	30
USA	7½	8½	9½	10½	11½	12½

Measurements approximate only; try before you buy.

numbers, with a lot of slink-ily cut black, are on offer.
☎ 06 678 9340 ✉ Via Condotti 8 ☼ 10am-7pm Mon-Sat, 2-7pm Sun Ⓜ Spagna

La Perla (4, F2)
Indulge your inner movie star with Italy's most famous range of lacy and luxurious underwear and nighties. Stiletto-heeled house slippers, luscious silk bras and delicious negligees to inject your life with va va voom. And guys remember: these make great presents for *both* of you.
☎ 06 699 41 933 ✉ Via Condotti 78 ☼ 3-7pm Mon, 10am-7.30pm Tue-Sat Ⓜ Spagna

Laura Biagiotti (4, F2)
Resembling an art gallery for clothes, this is the store of the queen of Roman fashion, with exquisitely made items for those red-carpet moments. The keen philanthropist and celebrated local is highly regarded for her luxurious knitwear, silk separates and superb detailing. If you need to ask the price you really shouldn't be shopping here.
☎ 06 679 12 05 ✉ Via Borgognona 43-44 ☼ 3.30-7.30pm Mon, 10.30am-7.30pm Tue-Sat Ⓜ Spagna

Lei (2, A1)
With funky clothes, pretty dresses, comic-strip prints and individual style, this is a shop for girls who like their style a little off-beat. It's mostly stocked with French designers but also has some local names. There's another branch at Via Nazionale 88.
☎ 06 687 54 32 ✉ Via dei Giubbonari 103 ☼ 10am-

2pm & 3.30-7pm Mon-Sat 🚌 to Largo Argentina 🚊 Via Arenula

Maga Morgana (4, D4)
This eclectic designer sells colourful knitwear and lots of unusual stuff, such as embroidered belts, woollen wraps or pretty, flimsy dresses, with an ethnic, hippie, boho influence. The nice thing is that it's not so overwhelming that it's off-putting.
☎ 06 68 79 995 ✉ Via del Governo Vecchio 27 & 98 ☼ 10am-1pm & 3-7.30pm 🚌 to Corso Vittorio Emanuelle II

MaxMara (4, F2)
Specialising in understated, classic modern tailoring for glamorous career women, and renowned for fine knitwear, MaxMara is one of Italy's top labels. Trademark items include classic jackets, trousers and suits, and superb winter coats in luxurious cashmere blends. **Max&Co** (4, F2) is the cheaper, less-dressy diffusion line at Via Condotti 46.
☎ 06 679 36 38 ✉ Via Frattina 28 ☼ 10am-7.30pm Mon-Sat Ⓜ Spagna

Only Hearts (4, D4)
A New York satellite in Rome, Only Hearts started off

Fabulous *fashionistas* face off on Via Frattina

SALES & BARGAINS!

Serious shoppers plan their holidays around the two seasonal sales, which usually take place from mid-January to mid-February, and for a month around August. Look for the *saldi* signs.

If you don't make it in time, do as the Romans do and bag some designer labels at an outlet – these are stores selling designer end-of-line and surplus stock at knock-down prices. These are mostly out of town, but in Rome try **Discount dell'Alta Moda** (4, F1; ☎ 06 361 37 96; Via Gesù e Maria 14 & 16; ☽ 10am-7.30pm), something of a graveyard for top-label fashion mistakes but with some gems if you rummage.

specialising in all things heart-shaped, but has branched out to other shapes, such as delectably frivolous underwear and unique, pretty women's clothes and accessories.
☎ 06 686 46 47 ✉ Piazza della Chiesa Nuova 21 ☽ 10am-8pm Tue-Sat, noon-8pm Sun, 4-8pm Mon 🚌 Corso Vittorio Emanuele II

Prada (4, F2)
Superstar Ms Prada presents understated but overwhelming style with retro-inspired, superbly cut, reassuringly expensive designs of impeccable quality with some quirky prints and stunning footwear.
☎ 06 679 08 97 ✉ Via Condotti 92 ☽ 10am-7pm Ⓜ Spagna

Scala Quattordici (4, D6)
This exquisite ladies tailor caters for film stars, royalty and the like-pursed. Also sells glamorous accessories to go with its one-off outfits.
☎ 06 588 35 80 ✉ Via della Scala 13 ☽ 9.30am-1.30pm Mon-Sat 4-8pm Tue-Sat 🚌 Viale di Trastevere

Valentino (4, F1)
King of Roman fashion, Valentino made his name dressing names like Sophia Loren and Audrey Hepburn and reached his peak in the '70s. But he's still a touchstone of Italian fashion, with his extraordinary tailoring and style.
☎ 06 679 58 62 ✉ Via Condotti 13 ☽ 10am-7pm Tue-Sat, 3-7pm Mon Ⓜ Spagna

Viviana Boutique (4, D4)
A treasure-trove boutique filled with edgy boho chic – all by young Italian designers, including Paola Frani who has a dedicated shop next door selling her delicate, crepe, chiffon and lace, often jewel-encrusted clothes. Lots of unusual, lovely pieces and some great shoes.
☎ 06 687 90 64 ✉ Via del Governo Vecchio 31 ☽ 10am-8pm 🚌 to Corso Vittorio Emanuelle II

Treat your feet to some artworks from Fausto Santini

SHOES & LEATHER GOODS

Italy is simply shoe heaven, and not-too-costly leather goods are among the things the beautiful country does best…along with food, fashion, football, coffee and corruption, of course.

Fancy yourself with a funky Mandarina Duck bag?

Fausto Santini (4, F2)
Fausto Santini's shoes are works of art. Italy's most original shoemaker's designs are quixotic, colourful and unlike any other. There are good men's brogues too. For bargains and previous seasons, check out the **outlet store** (5, A4; ☎ 06 488 09 34; Via Santa Maria Maggiore 165; 3.30-7.30pm Mon, 10am-1pm & 3.30-7.30pm Tue-Fri, 3-7.30pm Sat) near Cavour Metro.
☎ 06 678 41 14 ✉ Via Frattina 120 1-7pm Mon, 10am-7.30pm Tue-Sat, noon-7pm Sun Ⓜ Spagna

Francesco Biasia (4, G2)
Bag ladies form a beeline: Biasia designs gorgeous, well-crafted leather bags in jewel-like colours – arm-candy to die for and what's more, it's not outrageously priced.
☎ 06 679 27 27 ✉ Via Due Macelli 62 3.30-7pm Mon, 10am-7pm Tue-Sat Ⓡ Spagna

Furla (4, G2)
Next to the Spanish Steps is one of many Furla outlets, selling good-quality, high-fashion leather bags and accessories, in colours ranging from sweetie-bright to space-age metallic and grownup-neutral, including shoes, wallets, belts, sunglasses, watches and costume jewellery.
☎ 06 692 00 363 ✉ Piazza di Spagna 22 10am-8pm Ⓜ Spagna

Loco (6, B3)
Shoe fetishist *fashionistas* will go *loco* in Loco – among Rome's hippest shoe shops. More a trend-setter than fashion follower, it's small in size but big in attitude. Look out for United Nude creations.
☎ 06 688 08 216 ✉ Via dei Baullari 22 Ⓡ Corso Vittorio Emanuele II

Mandarina Duck (4, G2)
This place sells smart, funky, ergonomic luggage and bags with sharp Italian style that's as quirky as its name and signature discreet yellow duck logo, made from state-of-the-art technology fabrics or old-fashioned leather. There's another branch at Corso Victor Emmanuel II 16.
☎ 06 678 64 14 ✉ Via due Macelli 59 10am-7.30pm Mon-Sat Ⓜ Spagna

Nuyorica (6, B4)
Shoes as art: Rome's hippest shoe shop stocks cutting-edge international designers including Freelance, Ernesto Esposito, Rodolphe Menudier, Marc Jacobs, Chloe and Michel Perry. Exquisite and expensive, but your feet probably deserve it. There's another branch in TAD (see p61).
☎ 06 688 91 243 ✉ Piazza Pollarola 36-37 10am-7.30pm Mon-Sat Ⓡ to Corso Vittorio Emanuele II

Sciú Sciá (6, C3)
The owner of this shop sources the best shoes from designers around Italy then gets them made up for his stock. The designs are classic and contemporary, the expertly crafted shoes stylish and sturdy.
☎ 06 688 06 777 ✉ Via di Torre Argentina 8-9 3-7.30pm Mon, 10am-7.30pm Tue-Sat Ⓡ Largo Argentina

Tod's (4, F2)
Tod's understated men's and women's loafers are tremendously classic, comfortable and costly, ready to grace many an aristocratic weekend. Practical rubber studs on the back of the heel reduce those pesky driving scuffs.
☎ 06 678 68 28 ✉ Via Borgognona 45 10am-7.30pm Mon-Sat, 11am-2pm & 3-7.30pm Sun Ⓜ Spagna

ACCESSORIES & JEWELLERY

Bulgari (4, F2)

In a street filled with glitzy stores, Bulgari outglitzes them all. Italy's most prestigious jeweller displays its wares like museum exhibits, beautifully lit, accessible through its heavy glass Art Deco doors. They specialise in colourful stones set in both antique and chunky modern settings.
☎ 06 679 38 76 ✉ Via Condotti 10 ⏱ 3-7pm Mon, 10am-7pm Tue-Sat Ⓜ Spagna

La Cravatta su Misura (2, B3)

Glorious silks glow from the depths of this tiny Trastevere shop. Here you can buy the man who has everything a made-to-measure tie, stitched from the finest Italian silks and English wools. Choose your fabric, the width and length of the tie and, at a push, it can be ready in a few hours.
☎ 06 581 66 76 ✉ Via Santa Cecilia 12 ⏱ 10am-1pm & 4-7pm Mon-Sat 🚌 23, 280

Luisella Mariotti (4, F1)

With semi-precious stones, crystals, glass and nickel-free metals, Luisella Mariotta creates beautiful, delicate, spidery, out-of-this-world jewellery. Fantastic, original pieces abound in her small backstreet shop, at reasonable prices.
☎ 06 320 13 20 ✉ Via di Gesú e Maria 20 ⏱ 2.30-7.30pm Mon, 10.30am-7.30pm Tue-Sat Ⓜ Spagna

Millerighe (4, F3)

Upmarket, but not stratospherically so, Millerighe offers excellent quality shirts, ties, scarfs and cufflinks in a range of colours from conservative classics to after-dark disco that will give you a dash of Italian style.
☎ 06 699 204 50 ✉ Via del Gambero ⏱ 11.30am-7.30pm Mon, 10am-7.30pm Tue-Fri, 10am-8pm Sun 🚌 Via del Corso

Mondello Ottica (4, D4)

If you're in Rome, you need shades, and this is *the* place for the grooviest, quirkiest eyewear in town, with frames by leading European and international designers including Anne et Valentin, l.a.Eyeworks, Cutler and Gross, and the Belgian designer Theo. Prescription glasses can be ready the same day.
☎ 06 686 19 55 ✉ Via del Pellegrino 97-98 ⏱ 9.30am-1pm & 4-7.30pm Tue-Sat 🚌 to Corso Vittorio Emanuele II

Sermoneta (4, G2)

Butter-soft leather gloves in every possible colour, as well as other fabrics or with decorative stitching, lined with silk, cashmere, or angora. The assistants size up your hand with a canny glance and call for your exact size. But just try getting them to crack a smile.
☎ 06 679 19 60 ✉ Piazza di Spagna 61 ⏱ Mon-Sat 9.30am-8pm, Sun 10.30am-7pm Ⓜ Spagna

Tempi Moderni (6, A2)

Stunning vintage costume jewellery (especially Art Nouveau and Art Deco) is the speciality here: 19th-century resin brooches, Bakelite from the '20s and '30s, a glut of liquorice-allsort colours, and costume jewellery by couturiers such as Chanel, Dior and Balenciaga.
☎ 06 687 70 07 ✉ Via del Governo Vecchio 108 ⏱ 10am-1pm & 2-7.30pm Mon-Sat 🚌 to Corso Vittorio Emanuele II

Troncarelli (6, B3)

Italians really know how to wear hats, but don't fret, you can learn: this is where to get kitted out. A crammed little, somewhat grumpily staffed shop with all sorts of fetching headwear including bowlers, toppers, panamas, Borsalino and Florentine boaters.
☎ 06 687 93 20 ✉ Via della Cuccagna 15 ⏱ 9.30am-1pm & 3.30-7.30pm Mon-Sat 🚌 to Corso del Rinascimento

Can your credit card take it?

GIFTS & HOMEWARES

Artemide (4, F1)
For fabulous light fittings and lamps – from so minimalist you barely notice them to plastic pop statements – head here, to this accessible showroom with its dazzling stock displayed in artful niches.
☎ 06 360 01 802 ✉ Via Margutta 107 ⏱ 3-7pm Mon, 10am-1.30pm & 2.30-7pm Tue-Sat Ⓜ Flaminio, Spagna

C.U.C.I.N.A. (4, F2)
Stainless-steel design might no longer be where it's at but it still looks good in the *cucina* (kitchen). Alessi and other brands of high-quality kitchenware are stocked and ready to adorn your worktop.
☎ 06 679 12 75 ✉ Via Mario de' Fiori 65 ⏱ 3.30-7.30pm Mon, 10am-7.30pm Tue-Sat Ⓜ Spagna

De Sanctis (6, B2)
You can get a good selection of Alessi products and other designer kitchenware and tableware here – but best of all is the selection of sunny Italian ceramics, including the colourful work of the Sicilian ceramicist De Simone.
☎ 06 688 06 810 ✉ Piazza Navona 82/84 ⏱ 3.30-7.30pm Tue, 9.30am-1.30pm & 3.30-7.30pm Wed-Mon 🚌 to Corso di Rinascimento

Flos Arteluce (4, F2)
For your dramatic modern lighting and cutting-edge chandelier needs, get dazzled at Flos Arteluce, more a museum of lighting fixtures than a retail outlet.
☎ 06 320 76 31 ✉ Via del Babuino 84-85 ⏱ 3-7pm

Mon, 10am-7pm Tue-Fri, 10am-2pm Sat 🚌 Spagna

Leone Limentani (2, B1)
This fabulous rambling warehouse-style shop has an unbelievable choice of porcelain, glass and crystal, from the finest to bargain basement. It also stocks plenty of Alessi and a good selection of quality pots and pans.
☎ 06 688 06 686 ✉ Via Portico d'Ottavia 47 ⏱ 3.30-7.30pm Mon, 9.30am-1.30pm & 3.30-7.30pm Tue-Fri, 9am-7.30pm Sat 🚌 🚋 to Largo Argentina

Maurizio Grossi (4, F1)
In search of a bust of Marcus Aurelius or an obelisk for your desk? Then look no further. This marble emporium stocks heavy marble sculpture, including beautifully executed versions of Bernini's elephant, and inlaid tables perfect for the stately home.
☎ 06 360 01 935 ✉ Via Margutta 109 ⏱ 10am-1pm & 3.30-7.30pm Mon-Sat Ⓜ Flaminio, Spagna

Spazio Sette (6, C4)
Worth visiting as much for its interior – housed in a Renaissance *palazzo* – as for its wares, this is one of Rome's best homeware stores. Look

out for high-quality furniture, designer kitchen- and tableware and don't forget to look up at the gorgeous frescoed ceilings.
☎ 06 688 04 261 ✉ Via dei Barbieri 7 ⏱ 3.30-7.30pm Mon, 9.30am-1pm & 3.30-7.30pm Tue-Sat 🚌 🚋 to Largo Argentina

TAD (4, F1)
Spot design-conscious young Romans at TAD, a drop-dead-gorgeous mini-department store that stocks contemporary design – featuring lots of Perspex and exotically oriental influences. It also carries clothes and shoes from the hottest designers, music, homeware, flowers, unusual perfumes and fabric. There's a serene, über-chic (Italian-Thai) little café too (also sells cakes), with a courtyard.
☎ 06 326 95 131 🖥 www.taditaly.com ✉ Via del Babuino 155 ⏱ noon-7.30pm Mon, 10.30am-7.30pm Tue-Fri, 10.30am-8pm Sat, noon-8pm Sun Ⓜ Flaminio

TAX REFUNDS

A value-added tax of around 19%, known as IVA, is slapped onto just about everything in Italy. Non-EU residents, who spend more than €155 in the same shop on the same day, can claim a refund – when they leave the EU – on purchases from affiliated outlets displaying a 'Tax free for Tourists' sign. Complete a form in the shop and get it stamped by Italian customs as you leave. You can get an immediate cash refund at major airports.

MARKETS & MALLS

Borgo Parioli (3, D2)
North of centre in this wealthy residential district is a market selling original jewellery and accessories from the 1950s onwards – such as brooches, cigarette cases and watches – all in mint condition (but not always a bargain) as well as silverware, paintings, antique lamps and old gramophones.
☎ 06 855 27 73 ✉ Via Tirso 14 ☼ 9am-8pm 1st, 2nd & 3rd Sat & Sun of the month 🚌 63, 86 to Porta Pia 🚊 to Viale Regina Margherita

Galleria Alberto Sordi (4, F3)
A gracious covered shopping arcade, named after Rome's favourite actor, who died in 2003, this houses cafés and a good array of shops including Jam – a quirky department store; the Bridge – selling leather products; Tech it Easy – selling gadgets; Gusella (p65) – with children's clothes and toys; and a branch of Feltrinelli (p67).
✉ Piazza Colonna ☼ 10am-10pm 🚌 Via del Corso

Mercato delle Stampe (4, E3)
Browse the old prints and second-hand books at the Print Market and you might turn up early music scores, architectural engravings, chromo lithographs of fruit and flowers and views of Rome.
✉ Largo della Fontanella di Borghese ☼ 7am-1pm Mon-Sat 🚌 to Piazza Augusto Imperatore

Porta Portese (2, A3)
Rome's biggest, busiest and best-known market has thousands of stalls selling everything including the kitchen sink. It's mainly cheap clothes, shoes and accessories as well as furniture, knick knacks and all sorts of random items. You have to bargain or else it's boring. Watch out for pickpockets.
✉ btwn Piazza Porta Portese & Piazza Ippolito Nievo, parallel to Viale di Trastevere ☼ 7am-1pm Sun 🚌 to Viale Trastevere

Underground (4, G2)
This monthly subterranean market (held in a car park) has over 150 stalls selling antiques and collectables. There's a section for handmade goods and another stocked with clothes and toys for children.
☎ 06 360 05 345 ✉ Ludovisi underground car park, Via Francesco Crispi 96 ☼ 3-8pm Sat, 10.30am-7.30pm Sun 2nd weekend of the month Ⓜ Barberini

Via Sannio (3, D5)
Bargain new and vintage clothing, cheap jeans and leather in all its manifestations, are piled high at this bustling neighbourhood market – patient rummagers will pick up some real bargains.
✉ Via Sannio ☼ 8am-1pm Mon-Sat 🚌 to Piazza San Giovanni Ⓜ San Giovanni

Need a kitchen sink? Head straight for the Porta Portese

ARTS & ANTIQUES

Rome's fame as an antiques centre has pushed prices up to astronomical levels, and while you'll see lots of desirable pieces, bargains will be rare. The best places to look are the shops in and around Via dei Coronari (near Piazza Navona), Via Giulia and Via del Babuino. Via Margutta is in the long time artist's quarter, once home to Fellini. Today it resembles a more-picturesque South Kensington, lined with upmarket workshops and galleries.

Alinari (4, G2)
For evocative sepia prints, Alinari is the place. The Alinari brothers were famous late-19th-century Florentine photographers, and the prints (mostly views of Rome) and books on sale here are reproduced from the archives of their work, which contain more than a million glass-plate negatives.
☎ 06 679 29 23 ✉ Via Alibert 16a ☽ 3-7pm Mon, 9am-1pm & 3-7pm Tue-Sat Ⓜ Spagna

Animalier e Oltre (4, F1)
The attic of a family of wealthy eccentrics could look something like this, filled with curios and rustic furniture from northern Europe and America. Someone obviously has a penchant for animal-shaped antiques (including French 19th-century *animalier* sculptures). It's a treasure trove of weird and wonderful high-class bric-a-brac.
☎ 06 320 82 82 ✉ Via Margutta 47 ☽ 3.30-

7.30pm Mon, 9.30am-1pm & 3.30-7.30pm Tue-Sat Ⓜ Spagna

Comics Bazar (4, D4)
A rambling antique shop crammed with objects, lamps and furniture from the late 19th century to the 1940s, including a large selection of Viennese furniture by Thonet. And contrary to the name – no comics.
☎ 06 688 02 923 ✉ Via dei Banchi Vecchi 127-8 ☽ 9.30am-7.30pm Mon-

Sat 🚌 to Corso Vittorio Emanuele II

Nardecchia (6, B2)
This stately little shop offers splendid antique prints, including 18th-century etchings of Rome by Giovanni Battista Piranesi, and more inexpensive 19th-century views of the city.
☎ 06 686 93 18 ✉ Piazza Navona 25 ☽ 4.30-7.30pm Mon, 10am-1pm & 4.30-7.30pm Tue-Sun 🚌 to Corso di Rinascimento

Damsels in distress fear not – your knight awaits

FOOD & DRINK

In Italy, the humblest *alimentari* (grocery stores) can be a gourmet's delight. Wine, olive oil or grappa, jars of preserved vegetables or hunks of parmesan cheese are hard to resist (though check your country's customs regulations). The following shops offer something extra special.

Sample Italian vino delights. *Cin cin!*

Antica Norcineria Viola
(6, B4)
A penchant for pork? Make a beeline for this 19th-century establishment which sells everything but the pig's squeal. There's a huge range of dried and fresh sausage, rated as the best in Rome.
☎ 06 688 06 114
✉ Campo de' Fiori 43
🕔 7.30am-1.30pm & 3.30-8pm 🚌 🚃 to Largo Argentina

Castroni (4, B2)
Homesick expats head to this treasure-trove food hall for Marmite and Betty Crocker cake mixes, but this is also an Aladdin's cave of Italian specialities. You'll find oils, vinegars, spices, dried fruit, jams, sweets, chocolates – and that's just on the first shelf. There's also a café – a splendid pre-Vatican pit stop. There's another branch at Via di Porta Angelica.
☎ 06 687 43 83 ✉ Via Cola di Rienzo 196-8 🕔 8am-8pm Mon-Sat 🚌 to Piazza Risorgimento Ⓜ Ottaviano

Franchi (4, B2)
Look no further to fulfil all your cheese and salami needs, this wonderful delicatessen is piled high with delicious products. It's also famous for its takeaway tasty treats in case you can't wait till you get home.
☎ 06 687 46 51 🖥 www .franchi.it ✉ Via Cola di Rienzo 200 🕔 8.15am-9pm Mon-Sat Ⓜ Ottaviano

'Gusto (4, E2)
For the foodie in your life: this store, attached to the same-named, fabulous restaurant complex, sells food- and wine-related gifts: special olive oils, aged balsamic vinegars and condiments; wine, wine glasses, decanters and corkscrews; unusual kitchen appliances and implements; and lots of books.
☎ 06 322 62 73 ✉ Piazza Augusto Imperatore 7 🕔 10am-7.30pm 🚌 to Piazza Augusto Imperatore

Moriondo & Gariglio
(6, D2)
The delectable smell is the first thing you notice, then the old-fashioned glass cabinets filled with rows of chocolates and bon bons. Two pastry chefs from (chocolate-capital) Turin thrilled Romans when they brought their cocoa knack to town in 1886, and the current owner's father learned the craft from them.
☎ 06 699 08 56 ✉ Via del Piè di Marmo 21-2 🕔 9am-7.30pm Mon-Sat 🚌 🚃 to Largo Argentina

Volpetti (2, B5)
Go worship at this food shrine – one of Rome's best gourmet delis, with a superb selection of Italian cheeses. In Testaccio, it's a showcase for some of the finest foods in Italy and staff can give you background on why they are so special. Oils, vinegar, wine, grappa and pasta make good presents – you can organise international shipping via their website.
☎ 06 574 23 52 🖥 www .volpetti.com ✉ Via Marmorata 47 🕔 8am-2pm & 5-8.15pm Mon-Sat 🚌 🚃 to Via Marmorata Ⓜ Piramide

FOR CHILDREN

Al Sogno (6, B1)
A wonderland of toys, this is a gorgeous, upmarket toy shop, though its don't-touch, doll-heavy atmosphere makes it best for well-behaved girls.
☎ 06 686 41 98 ⊠ Piazza Navona 53 🕑 10am-8pm 🚌 to Corso del Rinascimento

Bartolucci (6, D1)
Tick-tocking clocks, pinewood planes, pinocchio signs, carved frames and figuerines, and myriad other articles make this shop a wooden wonderland.
☎ 06 691 908 94 ⊠ Via dei Pastini 98 🕑 9am-11pm daily 🚌 Largo Argentina

Bertè (6, B2)
This fun factory will send your kids giddy, with exquisite wooden dolls and puppets among its enchanting wares. A huge range here from rag dolls and games to nursery furnishings.
☎ 06 687 50 11 ⊠ Piazza Navona 107-11 🕑 3.30-7.30pm Mon, 9.30am-1pm & 3.30-7.30pm Tue-Sun 🚌 Corso del Rinascimento

Città del Sole (6, C1)
The best-quality educational and creative toys to stretch your budding genius and appeal to your inner child, at the city's best toyshop.
☎ 06 688 03 805 ⊠ Via della Scrofa 65 🕑 3.30-7.30pm Mon, 10am-7.30pm Tue-Sat 🚌 Corso del Rinascimento

Gusella (4, F3)
High-end kiddies clothes and shoes (aged 0-14), with stylish clobber (think Audrey Hepburn t-shirts and pink metallic shoes) that will leave your wallet feeling as light as a kite. There's a great toyshop in the basement, with some really imaginative, original games and toys that are much easier on the pocket.
☎ 06 679 39 80 ⊠ Galleria Angelo Sordi 24 🕑 10am-10pm 🚌 Via del Corso

La Cicogna (4, F2)
Dress your little darling in the latest from the big fashion houses and hang the expense. Choose here from Armani, D&G and other labels, as well as the shop's own prestigious brand.
☎ 06 678 69 77 ⊠ Via Frattina 138 🕑 noon-7.30pm Mon, 10am-7.30pm Tue-Sat, 11am-7pm Sun Ⓜ Spagna

Mel Giannino Stoppani Librerie per Ragazzi (6, F3)
Rome's best children's bookshop stocks around 15,000 Italian titles but one corner is devoted to French, Spanish, German and English books. There are some good toys, as well as a grown-up guidebook section. There's a convenient baby-changing area here too.
☎ 06 699 41 045 ⊠ Piazza dei Santissimi Apostoli 59-65 🕑 9.30am-7.30pm Mon-Sat, 10am-1pm & 4-7.30pm Sun 🚌 to Piazza Venezia

Shop for toys for your little Einstein in Città del Sole

Osh Kosh B'Gosh (4, G2)
Classic cute dungarees and other classy labourer-chic items for tiny tots. Osh Kosh have been in vogue since the '70s and look unlikely to fall out of fashion. This little store also sells appealing, quirky designs from Mini Metro, from denim skirts to frilled flares. ☎ 06 679 51 07 ⊠ Via di Propaganda 5 ⏱ 10am-3pm & 3.30-7.30pm Mon-Sat, 3.30-7.30pm Sun Ⓜ Spagna

BOOKS & MUSIC

Almost Corner Bookshop (2, A2)
A pocket-sized treasure trove stuffed floor-to-ceiling with a good selection of English titles, including bestsellers, contemporary literature, biography, history, travel guides, dictionaries and reference. ☎ 06 583 69 42 ⊠ Via del Moro 48 ⏱ 10am-1.30pm & 3.30-8pm, from 11am Sun, closes Sun in Aug 🚌 to Piazza Trilussa 🚊 to Viale di Trastevere

LITERARY ROME
Try Juvenal's *Satires* to explore ancient Rome's seedy side, Virgil's *Aeneid* about its beginnings or Goethe's *Italian Journey*, George Eliot's *Middlemarch* and Henry James' *Portrait of a Lady* and *Italian Hours* for a 19th-century take. A Capitoline statue inspired Nathanial Hawthorne's *Marble Faun*, while a good history is *Rome: Biography of a City* by Christopher Hibbert. Catch Georgina Masson's enthusiasm in her *Companion Guide to Rome* – the enduringly classic guidebook.

Anglo-American Bookshop (4, G2)
Novels, classics, reference books, literature and children's books – they're all here and all in English. There's also a good selection of travel guides and maps. ☎ 06 679 52 22 ⊠ Via della Vite 102 ⏱ 3.30-7.30pm Mon, 10am-7.30pm Tue-Sat Ⓜ Spagna

Disfunzioni Musicali (3, E4)
In the heart of San Lorenzo, this music store is the best for alternative, indie, rare, bootlegged and underground sounds. There's also a good range of second-hand vinyl and CDs, local and international, from opera to rock. ☎ 06 446 19 84 ⊠ Via degli Etruschi 4-14 ⏱ 3-8pm Mon,

Books, books and more books at the Anglo-American Bookshop

0.30am-8pm Tue-Sat 🚌 to Via Tiburtina

Feltrinelli (6, C3)
If it's in Italian and in print, Feltrinelli will have it. Rome's biggest bookshop has a huge range of nonfiction books – art, photography, cinema, food and history among other subjects – as well as an extensive selection of Italian literature, travel guides, maps and titles in English.
☎ 06 688 03 248 ✉ Via di Torre Argentina 5a 🕙 9am-9pm Mon-Fri, 9am-11pm Sat, 9am-8pm Sun 🚌 🚋 to Largo Argentina

Feltrinelli International (4, J3)
Depending on your mother tongue, this multilingual shop stocks *livres, libros, livros, bücher,* books or *libri* – contemporary literature and classics, fiction and nonfiction, plus lots of guidebooks for Rome, Italy and the rest of the world.
☎ 06 482 78 78 ✉ Via VE Orlando 84 🕙 9am-8pm Mon-Sat, 10am-1.30pm & 4-7.30pm Sun 🚇 Repubblica

Libreria del Viaggiatore (6, A3)
A charming pocket-sized store devoted to travel, stacked floor to ceiling with a splendid range of guides and travel literature in various languages, and a huge range of maps.
☎ 06 688 01 048 ✉ Via del Pellegrino 78 🕙 10am-2pm & 4-8pm 🚌 to Corso Vittorio Emanuele II

Lion Bookshop (4, F2)
Fabulous long-running English-language bookshop

with a good children's section and a peaceful café that's handy for a tranquil cuppa.
☎ 06 688 01 048 ✉ Via dei Greci 33 🕙 10am-7.30pm Mon-Sat, 3.30-7.30pm Sun 🚇 Spagna

Messaggerie Musicali (4, F2)
Rome's largest music store has three levels of everything from Italian golden oldies to the most recent chart 'offerings' (and lots of fluff in between). Also sells an excellent range of international magazines.
✉ Via del Corso 472 🕙 10am-8pm 🚌 to Via del Corso

Soul Food (5, A6)
Vintage, imported and rare vinyl is what this shop is all about. Trainspotters will spend happy hours rummaging through the beautifully displayed stock. Also sells CDs and posters.
☎ 06 704 520 25 ✉ Via di San Giovanni in Laterano 192 🕙 10.30am-1.30pm & 3.30-8pm Tue-Sat 🚌 Piazza San Giovanni in Laterano 🚇 San Giovanni

SPECIALIST SHOPS

Ai Monasteri (6, B1)
So this is how monks pay the rent: step back in time at this atmospheric wood-panelled shop selling herbal essences, spirits, soaps, balms, deodorants, anti-wrinkle creams, bubble bath and various liqueurs made by monks in abbeys throughout Italy.
☎ 06 688 02 783 🖳 www .monasteri.it ✉ Corso del Rinascimento 72 🕙 10am-

7.30pm Mon-Wed & Fri-Sat, 10am-1pm Thu 🚌 to Corso del Rinascimento

L'Olfattorio (4, E1)
Set out like a modern bar but with perfume instead of drink, L'Olfattorio doesn't actually sell anything. Instead it offers scent-smellings. Choose a scent from the bottles of perfume (labelled by ingredient) on the wall, try it, and if you find something you like, the bartender will tell you what it's called and where you can buy it. Smellings are free but bookings are appreciated.
☎ 06 361 23 25 ✉ Via di Ripetta 34 🕙 3.30-7.30pm Tue-Sat 🚇 Flaminio

Officina della Carta (4, D5)
This tiny Trastevere workshop makes beautiful hand-printed storage boxes, photo albums, recipe books, notepads, photo frames and diaries, and some beautiful paper theatres – all of which make terrific gifts.
☎ 06 589 55 57 ✉ Via Benedetta 26b 🕙 9.30am-1pm & 4-7.30pm 🚌 to Piazza Trilussa 🚋 to Viale di Trastevere

A medieval shopping list?

Eating

Food glorious food. Romans love to eat, and to eat together with lots of cheerful noisy chatter. The table is the firm foundation of Italian life and you don't have to look far to get a good meal in any price range, with many traditional trattorie, atmospheric *enoteche* (winebars serving food) and increasing numbers of stylish restaurants to whom décor means more than a candle stuffed in an empty bottle of Chianti. The only thing to watch out for is around main tourist sights, where you can get overcharged for an underwhelming meal. Near a major monument it pays to follow a guidebook, look out for local restaurant-guide stickers, or take a recommendation.

Eat like an Italian

Italians rarely eat a sit-down *colazione* (breakfast), preferring a cappuccino and *cornetto* (croissant) at a bar. For *pranzo* (lunch) or *cena* (dinner), a full meal consists of antipasto, such as bruschetta or prosciutto (cured ham) with melon or figs, a *primo piatto*, usually pasta, followed by the *secondo* of meat or fish. No one will look askance if you plump for a *primo or* a *secondo* – most Romans will be doing the same. You order an *insalata* (salad) or *contorno* (side dish) separately, and the meal is rounded off with *dolce* (dessert), *gelato* (ice cream) or fruit and *caffè*, and often a digestive – *amaro* (herbal liqueur), grappa or *limoncello*.

OPEN IN AUGUST?

Many restaurants close for at least a few weeks over August, so before making a trek in midsummer, give your destination a call.

QUANTO COSTA?

The pricing symbols used indicate the cost of a three-course meal (antipasto, *primo* and *secondo*) à la carte, excluding drinks.

€	under €20
€€	€20–30
€€€	€30–45
€€€€	over €45

Bills usually include *pane e coperto* (a cover charge), which ranges from €1 to €5 per person. Service is usually added to your bill – if in doubt, ask. Additional tipping is at your discretion; Italians often don't bother leaving anything but tourists are expected to leave 10% or at least round up the bill.

Tasty snacks in an amazing setting – Piazza della Rotunda and the Pantheon

CAMPO DE' FIORI

The buzzing area around Il Campo, which is particularly popular after dark, is packed with restaurants, with some real gems thrown in.

Enjoy a classic Roman pasta at Da Sergio

Ar Galletto (6, A4)
Trattoria €€
Sublimely located on the corner of Piazza Farnese, this has solid, excellent Roman fare overseen by cheery waiters. Outside seats can't be beat but the lemon-yellow interior is a mellow place for a long meal.
☎ 06 686 17 14 ⊠ Piazza Farnese 102 🕑 12.15-3pm & 7.30-11pm Mon-Sat 🚌 ⓖ

Da Sergio (2, A1)
Trattoria €
This splendid, typical (gingham tablecloths, busy waiters, strings of garlic) trattoria offers hearty portions of Roman pasta classics. Its loyal following doesn't bother with menus. In summer tables line the narrow alley.
☎ 06 686 42 93 ⊠ Vicolo delle Grotte 27 🕑 12.30-3pm & 6.30pm-midnight Mon-Sat 🚌 Largo Argentina ⓖ Ⓥ

Ditirambo (6, B3)
Trattoria €€
Charming, intimate Ditirambo is a sophisticated, much-applauded take on the trattoria. Food is delicious, innovative and mostly organic, with good vegetarian choices. Across the road is similarly special sister restaurant, Grappolo d'Oro.
☎ 06 687 16 26 ⊠ Piazza della Cancelleria 72

🕑 1-3pm & 7.20-11.30pm Tue-Sun 🚌 Corso Vittorio Emanuele II ⓖ Ⓥ

Filetti di Baccalà (2, A1)
Trattoria €
On a tiny scooter-strewn piazza, 'Fillet of Cod' does just as it says above the door, specialises in deep-fried *baccalà*. It's the Roman equivalent of fish and chips, without the chips.
☎ 06 686 40 18 ⊠ Largo dei Librari 88 🕑 6-10.30pm Mon-Sat 🚌 🚋 to Largo Argentina ⓖ

Forno di Campo de' Fiori (6, A3)
Pizza a taglio €
Refuel with a slice of pizza at a Roman favourite. Try *pizza rossa* or *bianca* (with or without tomato sauce), drizzled

with olive oil and sprinkled with crunchy sea salt. You can see it being swung in out of the ovens next door. Also sells good cakes.
☎ 06 688 06 662 ⊠ Campo de' Fiori 22 🕑 7am-1.30pm & 5.30-8pm Mon-Wed, Fri & Sat, 7am-1.30pm Thu 🚌 🚋 to Largo Argentina ⓖ Ⓥ

L'Angelo Divino (2, A1)
Enoteca €€
A tucked-away find, this divine angel of wine offers splendid vino accompanied by a fine array of cheeses, meats, fish and other snacks, in cosy wood- and bottle-lined rooms.
☎ 06 686 44 13 ⊠ Via dei Balestrari 12 🕑 10am-2.30pm & 5pm-2am Tue-Sun 🚌 Largo Argentina Ⓥ

SONO VEGETARIANA/O

Vegetarians will have the choice of an abundance of antipasti (before pasta) and suitable pasta dishes, as well as pizzas. Be mindful of hidden ingredients – check that it's *senza carne o pesce* (without meat or fish).

Dedicated veggie places include the swish Il Margutta RestorArte (p75) and **Arancia Blu** (3, E4; ☎ 06 445 41 05; Via dei Latini 55-65) and the less-formal **Naturist Club – L'Isola** (4, F3; ☎ 06 679 25 09; 4th fl, Via della Vite 14). You'll also find plenty of choice at restaurants where you see the Ⓥ symbol.

Renato e Luisa (6, C4)
Trattoria €€
A lively young crowd packs this backstreet trattoria. The décor is simple, and the cooking complex, with a buttery French twist. Try the delicious starter of goat's cheese with walnuts and honey. Expect haphazard service when busy. ☎ 06 68 69 660 ✉ Via dei Barbieri 25 🕑 8.30pm-midnight Tue-Sun 🚍 Largo Argentina ⚹

GHETTO & CAPITOLINE

The Ghetto's extremely narrow crumbling-ochre streets are a culinary hotspot and the place to savour Roman-Jewish cuisine, while Capitoline Hill has Rome's best café-with-a-view.

Capitoline Museum Café (2, C1)
Café €€
This amazing terrace overlooking Rome is a well-kept secret, hidden away behind the museum, and accessible from the piazza even if you haven't done the cultural bit. ☎ 06 691 90 564 ✉ Piazza del Campidoglio 🕑 9am-7.30pm Tue-Sun 🚍 to Piazza Venezia ♿ excellent (only through museum) ⚹ Ⓥ

Da Giggetto (2, B1)
Trattoria €€€
A wonderful ghetto labyrinth specialising in Roman-Jewish cuisine, with glorious deep-fried *carciofi* (artichoke). Best to bag an outside table with views over 1st-century Portico d'Ottavia. ☎ 06 686 11 06 ✉ Via del Portico d'Ottavia 🕑 12-3pm

& 7.30-11pm Tue-Sun 🚍 Via Arenula ♿ good ⚹

Il Forno del Ghetto (2, B1)
Bakery €
Spot this hole-in-the-wall Jewish bakery by the queue. Venerable ladies sell kosher warm almond and cinamon biscuits, and (very) hard and soft fruit cakes. ☎ 06 688 03 012 ✉ Piazza Costaguti 30-31 🕑 8am-2.30pm & 3-8pm Mon-Fri, 8am-2.30pm Sat & Sun 🚍 to Piazza Venezia ⚹ Ⓥ

La Taverna degli Amici (2, B1)
Ristorante €€€
On a quintessential ivy-draped piazza surrounded by burnt-orange buildings, this is a lovely restaurant, worlds away from nearby noisy Piazza Venezia. Your typical Roman classics are on the menu, with many excellent accompanying wines. ☎ 06 699 20 637 ✉ Piazza Margana 36 🕑 12.30-3pm & 7.30-midnight Tue-Sun 🚍 to Piazza Venezia ⚹ Ⓥ

Piperno (2, B1)
Ristorante €€€€
Here white-clad waiters pander to desires involving deep-fried veggies, mozzarella and *baccalà*. Traditional but unstuffy, it's ideal for leisurely lunches or family occasions, although eating *palle del nonno* ('grandpa's balls', ricotta and chocolate puffs) might make some feel uneasy. ☎ 06 688 06 629 ✉ Via Monte de' Cenci 9 🕑 12.30-2.30pm & 8.30-10.30pm Tue-Sat, 12-3pm Sun (booking required Sun) 🚍 to Via Arenula ⚹

Sora Margherita (2, B1)
Trattoria €
With no sign, Sora Margherita feels like you've been let in on a secret. It's a bustling old-style, rough-and-ready favourite, offering hearty Roman and Jewish dishes served on Formica table tops. Try the deep-fried artichoke. Book or queue. ☎ 06 687 42 16 ✉ Piazza delle Cinque Scole 30 🕑 noon-3pm Mon-Fri summer, noon-3pm Tue-Sun winter 🚍 to Via Arenula ⚹ Ⓥ

Another little artichoke is served in the ghetto, Da Giggetto

PANTHEON & PIAZZA NAVONA

The *centro storico* (historic city centre) teems with places – the best tend to be tucked away in sidestreets rather than on the main squares.

Alfredo e Ada (4, D4)
Trattoria €

Aunt Ada's been shuffling between the few tables of this popular joint for over 50 years. No sign, no coffee, no menu; just set meals – chalked on a board if you're lucky – of simple pastas and Roman staples like *salsiccia con fagioli* (sausage with beans).
☎ 06 687 88 42 ✉ Via dei Banchi 14 🕒 noon-3pm & 7.30pm-midnight Mon-Fri 🕭

Casa Bleve (6, C3)
Enoteca €€€

While away an afternoon in a stately column-lined courtyard, roofed with stained glass. At this upmarket *enoteca* the choice of wines is spectacular and you choose your food from an Epicurean spread of cold cuts.
☎ 06 686 59 70 ✉ Via del Teatro Valle 48-49 🕒 12.30-3pm & 7-10pm Wed-Fri, 12.30-3pm Tue & Sat 🚌 Largo Argentina 🕭 excellent Ⓥ

Cul de Sac (6, A2)
Enoteca €€

Off Piazza Navona, this *enoteca* has long been serving up great wines and snacks. There's a little outside deck or cramped indoor seating, and knowledgeable waiters to talk you through the menu.

NICE ICE

You'll find wonderful ice cream all over the place – a handy tip is to check the pistachio: bright green = bad; earthy ochre = good.

Best-in-Rome contenders include delectable San Crispino (p81), historic Giolitti (p72), and Gelateria della Palma (right) with a bamboozling choice. La Fonte della Salute (p79) in Trastevere offers big helpings and guiltfree portions of frozen yogurt. Tre Scalini (p74) is famous for its *tartufo nero* (black truffle) while dissolute-seeming Bar San Calisto (p88) has surprisingly splendid chocolate *gelato*.

On summer nights Romans favour *grattacecca* – crushed ice with a choice of fruity sauces – served from Tiber-side kiosks.

Good *primi* and *secondi* include splendid red lentil soup and tasty Roman meatballs.
☎ 06 688 01 094 ✉ Piazza Pasquino 73 🕒 noon-4pm, 6pm-12.30am Mon-Sat 🚌 to Corso Rinascimento 🕭

Da Francesco (6, A2)
Pizzeria €

Traditional, atmospheric and friendly, this is a classic wham-bam pizzeria filled with a boisterous, cheerful crowd of Romans and tourists tucking into tasty and typical pizzas, seating indoors or out.
☎ 06 686 40 09 ✉ Piazza del Fico 29 🕒 12.30-3pm, 7.30pm-1am (closed Tue lunch) 🚌 to Corso Vittorio Emanuele II Ⓥ 🕭

Enoteca Corsi (6, D3)
Enoteca €

Merrily worse-for-wear, at old-devil Corsi plentiful food is served in a busy arched room. The menu – written (in Italian) on a board as you enter – follows the Roman gastronomic calendar so if it's gnocchi, it's Thursday.
☎ 06 679 08 21 ✉ Via del Gesù 87-88 🕒 noon-3pm Mon-Sat 🚌 to Piazza Venezia 🕭

Gelateria della Palma (6, C1)
Gelateria €

It's a bit touristy, but what's not to like when it's an ice-cream version of Willy Wonka's chocolate factory,

with 100 or so dazzling flavours. House speciality is the extra creamy mousse.
☎ 06 688 06 752 ⊠ Via della Maddalena 20 ⏱ 8am-1am 🚌 to Largo Argentina ♿ 🅥

Giolitti (6, D1)
Gelateria €

All woodpanels and frosted glass, this stuck-in-time place is Rome's most famous gelataria. Gregory Peck and Audrey Hepburn swung past in *Roman Holiday*, and it used to deliver to Pope John Paul II.
☎ 06 699 12 43 ⊠ Via degli Uffici del Vicario 40 ⏱ 7am-1am 🚌 to Corso Rinascimento ♿ 🅥

Divine ice cream from Giolitti

Green Tea (6, D2)
Oriental €€€

It's rare to find a good Chinese restaurant here, and this is something different from the special-fried bog-standard: a restaurant, tea room and boutique, with immaculate attention to detail and excellent oriental food. An oasis.
☎ 06 679 86 28 ⊠ Via del Pié di Marmo 28 ⏱ 1-2.45pm & 7.40-11pm Mon-Sat 🚌 🚋 to Largo Argentina 🅥

Il Bacaro (4, E3)
Ristorante €€€

Gorgeously intimate Il Bacaro is in a characteristic cobbled corner of Rome, and has outstanding grub – exquisite risotto, pasta and *secondi*. Summer seating is vine-shaded in the little square. Booking is recommended.
☎ 06 686 41 10 ⊠ Via degli Spagnoli 27 ⏱ 12.30-2.30pm & 7.45pm-midnight Mon-Sat 🚌 to Corso Rinascimento 🅥

Il Convivio di Troiano (4, E3)
Ristorante €€€€

Michelin-starred Il Convivio, set in a 16th-century building, is elegant, intimate and impeccable. It's a foodie delight: memorable dishes and a choice of 2000 bottles from the wine cellar. An attitude of hushed reverence is recommended.
☎ 06 686 94 32 🖥 www.ilconviviotroiani.com ⊠ Vicolo dei Soldati 31 ⏱ 8-11pm Mon-Sat 🚌 to Corso Rinascimento 🅥

THE BEST COFFEE & CAFÉS

Italy has the world's best coffee. Espresso (a short black) is most popular – simply ask for '*un caffè*'. A *caffè doppio* is a double and may catapult you through the window. A *caffè americano* is just for tourists: a long, watered-down espresso. A *corretto* is an espresso 'corrected' with grappa. A *caffè latte* is milky, a *caffè macchiato* is an espresso with a dash of milk and a *latte macchiato* is the reverse. A cappuccino is an espresso with foamed milk, and the favoured morning drink. Romans never drink milky coffee after, say, 11am and anyone who does is, well, a bit odd.

Rome's best coffee is the *gran caffè* at **Caffè Sant'Eustachio** (6, C2; Piazza Sant'Eustachio 82), made to a secret recipe and guaranteed to put the zing in your sightseeing. Specify you want it bitter (*amaro*) or with little sugar (*poco zucchero*) or it'll be sweeter than sweet.

La Tazza D'Oro (6, D1, Via degli Orfani 84) is a lovely stand-up stop that's been going since 1946 and feels it, glimmering with burnished fittings. It's famed for its *granite al caffè con panna* (crushed ice coffee with cream) in summer.

Caffè Greco (p74) is from another age, at Caffè Canova-Tadolini (p76) you are surrounded by sculpture, Ciampini al Caffè du Jardin (p74) has views, and at **Caffè Farnese** (6, A4; Piazza Farnese) you can watch the world go by.

La Focaccia (6, A1)
Ristorante/Café €€

In winter, look for the glow of the pizza oven on this fashionable street; the dining rooms are downstairs. In summer nab one of the scarce outside tables, stunningly overlooked by Santa Maria della Pace.

☎ 06 688 03 312 ⊠ Via della Pace 11 ⏰ noon–12.30am 🚌 to Corso Vittorio Emanuele II Ⓥ

La Rosetta (6, C1)
Ristorante €€€€

Rosetta is so excellent it doesn't have to be overly formal. Outside you can glimpse the Pantheon but it's better to sit inside amid yellow hues and crisp white table linens to concentrate on the simple dishes prepared with genius.

☎ 06 686 10 02 ⊠ Via Rosetta 8–9 ⏰ 12.45–2.45pm & 7.30–11pm Mon–Sat 🚌 to Via del Corso

Lo Zozzone (6, A2)
Pizza a taglio €

Lo Zozzone – the 'dirty one' (a nickname that stuck) – is a central gem: pay at the till for a belly-filling regular (€2.50) or a belly-busting large (€3)

pizza *bianca*, then ask for it to be filled with your heart's desire from the bar.

☎ 06 688 085 75 ⊠ Via del Teatro Pace 32 ⏰ 9am–9pm Mon–Fri, 9am–11pm Sat 🚌 to Corso Rinascimento

Maccheroni (6, C1)
Trattoria €€

In one of Rome's fashionable corners, this simple, classy trattoria – with pale bottle-lined walls – has a certain buzz. It gets packed with a trendy twenty- and thirty-something crowd gossiping over traditional Roman dishes.

☎ 06 683 07 895 ⊠ Piazza delle Coppelle 44 ⏰ 1–3pm & 7.30–11.30pm Mon–Sat 🚌 to Corso Rinascimento Ⓥ

Obiká (4, E3)
Mozzarella Bar €€

Obiká ('here it is' in Neapolitan dialect) is a mozzarella bar, offering the finest white stuff (fresh daily) and other fabulous products. Décor is ancient meets modern, with columns and an underlit floor.

☎ 06 683 26 30 ⊠ Piazza di Firenze ⏰ noon–midnight 🚌 to Corso Rinascimento ♿ Ⓥ

Osteria del Sostegno (6, D1)
Ristorante €€

Here you have stumbled on an insider secret. It's intimate, popular with journalists and politicians, in a tucked-away corner, with a tiny canopied terrace. Food is smashing. Papa's place, **Ristorante Settimio** (6, C1; ☎ 06 678 96 51; Via delle Colonnelle 14) up the road is just as good.

☎ 06 679 38 42 ⊠ Via delle Colonnelle ⏰ 12.30–3pm & 7.30–11pm 🚌 to Largo Argentina

Pizzeria da Baffetto (4, D4)
Pizzeria €

One of Rome's best, rowdiest and cheapest pizzerias. It's full of loud, cheerful Romans and less-loud, cheerful tourists tucking into terrific thin-crust pizzas with charred edges and simple toppings, bashed down by waiters on a mission. You'll have to queue and share tables.

☎ 06 686 16 17 ⊠ Via del Governo Vecchio 114 ⏰ 7pm–1am 🚌 to Corso Rinascimento ♿ Ⓥ

Try to nab an outside table at La Focaccia

Riccioli Café (6, C1)
Japanese €€€

Famous for fish: go for some sushi and sashimi (or even ostrich) at this fashionable spot, seated on blue-velvet banquettes under a dramatic tangled sculptural lampshade or a beautiful chandelier made of discarded plastic bottles.
☎ 06 682 10 313 ⊠ Via del Coppelle 10a
🕙 10am-2am 🚌 to Corso Rinascimento Ⓥ

Fancy some fish? Try Riccioli Café

Tre Scalini (6, B2)
Café €€€

Turn your Piazza Navona stroll into a revelation by sampling a Tre Scalini *tartufo nero* (black truffle) – a rich chocolate *gelato* ball, filled with huge chocolate chunks, served with whipped cream. As a satisfied punter put it: 'this must be what darkness tastes like.'
☎ 06 688 01 996 ⊠ Piazza Navona 30 🕙 8-1am Thu-Tue 🚌 Corso Rina ♿ fair 👶 Ⓥ

TRIDENTE

The upmarket shopping district of Tridente has some great restaurants and evocative cafés.

Antica Enoteca (4, F2)
Enoteca €€

Local shopkeepers and shoppers keep this Roman institution packed. The 19th-century fittings include an impressive cash desk and a long counter ideal for sampling wines until you feel ready for some fab food served at the rear tables.
☎ 06 679 08 96 ⊠ Via della Croce 76b 🕙 10am-1am 🚌 to Via del Corso Ⓜ Spagna

Babington's (4, G2)
Café €€€€

If you want to make like you're on a Grand Tour, stop off at this more-English-than-the-English tearoom. Opened by the Babington sisters for homesick 19th-century travellers, it's popular with a genteel set, digging into genteel teas.
☎ 06 678 60 27 ⊠ Piazza di Spagna 23 🕙 9am-8.15pm Wed-Sun Ⓜ Spagna ♿ good 👶 Ⓥ

Café Greco (4, G2)
Café €€€

A famous literary haunt. All red-flock, gilt mirrors and penguin waiters, illustrious figures popping in for a cuppa have included Casanova, Stendhal, Wagner, Goethe and Byron. Now it's frequented by well-heeled shoppers (prices reflect this).
☎ 06 679 17 00 ⊠ Via Condotti 86 🕙 10.30am-7pm Mon & Sun, 9am-7pm Tue-Sat Ⓜ Spagna Ⓥ

Ciampini al Caffè du Jardin (4, F1)
Café €€

Get dreamy over fabulous views at this hidden-away greenery-surrounded café near the top of the Spanish Steps. It's ideal for a sunset snack or *aperitivo*.
☎ 06 678 5678 ⊠ Viale Trinitá de' Monti 🕙 8am-8pm Thu-Tue Apr–mid-Oct, to 1am mid-May–mid-Sep Ⓜ Spagna 👶 Ⓥ

THE APERITIVO HOUR

Milan's hippest import is the *aperitivo*, a favourite social activity of fashionable young Romans. Many bars offer a buffet from around 6pm to 9pm – either free with your drink or you pay a dedicated charge for a drink and snacks. If you have enough helpings, you might not even need to eat dinner. Some of the best and most happening spots for an *aperitivo* are Crudo (p88), Opera (p89), Freni e Frizioni (p89), Zest (p90), Obiká (p73), Bibli (p78) and Ferrara (p78).

Dal Bolognese (4, E1)
Ristorante €€€€
Beautiful people decorate this perennially über-chic restaurant on one of Rome's finest squares. Inside is wood-panelled and filled with exotic flowers; food is simple and exquisite – mostly Emilia-Romagna dishes – recommended are tagliatelle with ragú, and tuna tartare.
☎ 06 361 14 26 ☒ Piazza del Popolo 1 ⏲ 12.30-3pm & 8.15-11pm Tue-Sun Ⓜ Flaminio

GiNa (4, F2)
Café €€
Delightfully white, with glowing white lights and comfy white seats, this is hidden near Spagna and ideal for dropping into once you've shopped, with a great range of soups, salads, cakes and panini. Borghese Park picnics (€35 for two) are also provided.
☎ 06 678 02 51 ☒ Via San Sebastianello 7A ⏲ 11am-10pm Tue-Sun, 11am-5pm Mon Ⓜ Spagna ♿ Ⓥ

'Gusto (4, E2)
Pizzeria/Ristorante €€
More New York than Rome, this mould-breaking gastronomic emporium is what Terence Conran might dream up if he were Italian, with outside seating to see and be seen at, huge illuminated flowerpots, and a warehouse-like interior. It comprises a popular pizzeria, restaurant, enoteca and kitchen shop.
☎ 06 322 62 73 ☒ Piazza Augusto Imperatore 9 ⏲ ristorante12.45-3pm & 7.45pm-midnight, pizzeria 12.30-3pm & 7.30pm-1am, enoteca 11am-2am 🚌 to Piazza Augusto Imperatore ♿ Ⓥ

Il Margutta RistorArte (4, F1)
Vegetarian €€
On a gallery-lined street, vegetarian-with-style Il Margutta is red, black and white, with long, curved sofas. Food is fab and brunch is particularly good (€15 with a choice of up to 50 dishes).
☎ 06 326 50 577 ☒ Via Margutta 118 ⏲ 12.30-3pm & 7.30-11pm Mon-Sat Ⓜ Spagna, Flaminio ♿ Ⓥ

Il Palazzetto (4, G2)
Champagne & Wine Bar €€€
A little terrace café overlooking the top of the Spanish Steps, this location can't be beat on a sunny day, ideal for a glass of spumante under red and white sunshades. They mainly serve salads and cold meats, but will whip up pasta on request.
☒ Hassler Villa Medici ⏲ noon-4pm Tue-Sat ♿ Ⓥ

Le Pain Quotidien (4, E2)
Café €€
A Belgian outpost selling delicious tarts, sandwiches and pastries. It might not be Roman but Romans adore it and it's a great stop for refuelling between sights, with big arched rooms, lots of ash wood and big communal tables.
☎ 06 688 077 27 ☒ Via Tomacelli 24-25 ⏲ 9am-midnight Wed-Mon, 9am-7.30pm Tue 🚌 to Via del Corso ♿ Ⓥ

It's a struggle to choose just one dish at Il Margutta RestorArte

Museo Atelier Canova Tadolini (4, F2)

Café-Ristorante €€€

In 1818 sculptor Canova signed a contract for this studio that agreed it would be forever preserved for sculpture. Still stuffed with statues, it's where to go for swanky tea, snacks, *aperitivo* (€8) or a full meal towered over by huge maquettes. ☎ 06 321 107 02 ⊠ Via del Babuino 150A/B ⏱ 8am-8.30pm Mon-Sat Ⓜ Spagna Ⓥ

Osteria Margutta (4, F2)

Trattoria €€€

In the upmarket artists' quarter, this discreet trattoria is fronted by a flood of greenery. Inside is theatrical and pretty, all rich reds, blue glass and fringed lampshades. Plaques on chairs testify to famous thespian bums they have supported. ☎ 06 323 10 25 ⊠ Via Margutta 82 ⏱ 12.30-3pm & 7.30-midnight Mon-Sat Ⓜ Spagna Ⓥ

LET'S DO BRUNCH

A recent foodie phenomenon is the brunch. Many places offer special brunch menus or buffets at the weekend, usually served about lunchtime rather than shortly post-breakfast. These would be great for soaking up after the night before, if Romans actually got drunk, but anyway, they offer a different menu of yummy breakfast-style foods (pancakes and elaborate snacks). Best places to go when you have a brunch-like hankering are Opera (p89), Obiká (p73), Bibli (p78), 'Gusto (p75), Il Margutta RistorArte (p75), Café Café (opposite) and Le Pain Quotidien (p75).

Palatium (4, F2)

Trattoria €€

Modern, slick and artfully lit, Palatium is an unusually contemporary-looking *enoteca*, which promotes Lazio produce and wines. You can taste local wines while eating excellent food, including specialities such as *porchetta* (ham roasted with herbs). ☎ 06 692 02 132 ⊠ Via Frattina 94 ⏱ 11am-11pm Mon-Sat Ⓜ Spagna ♿ excellent Ⓥ

Ristorante Matricianella (4, F2)

Trattoria €€

A tranquil trattoria off pretty Piazza Lucina, with blue-and-white checked tablecloths, a porcelain-laden fresco, and some outside tables. Expect good service, great fried snacks, excellent meat dishes, and delicious chocolate and ricotta dessert. Book ahead. ☎ 06 683 21 00 ⊠ Via del Leone 4 ⏱ 12.30-3pm & 7.30pm-1am Mon-Sat Ⓜ Spagna

Like looking upon a stage – inside Osteria Margutta

AROUND THE COLOSSEUM & APPIA ANTICA

The Colosseum area has some excellent backstreet finds, while Appia Antica is dotted with pleasant restaurants and cafés, with one outstanding choice.

Crates of fresh fruit are available on street corners

Café Café (4, J6)
Café €€
So good they named it twice, this a terrific local gem to escape the throng and chill out over international newspapers, with an ever-changing array of salads, light meals, sandwiches and Sunday brunch.
☎ 06 700 87 43 ✉ Via dei Santi Quattro 44 ⏱ 11am-1.30am, lunch noon-3.45pm dinner 7.30-11.30pm Thu-Tue Ⓜ Colosseo ♿ Ⓥ

Cavour 313 (4, H5)
Enoteca €
A dark wood-lined *enoteca* with an almost pub-like cosiness, Cavour 313 remains deeply traditional and popular for its long wine list and tasty accompaniments (cold cuts, pasta dishes and so on).
☎ 06 678 54 96 ✉ Via Cavour 313 ⏱ 12.30-2.30pm & 7.30pm-12.30am Mon-Sat, 7.30pm-12.30am Sun Ⓜ Colosseo ♿ Ⓥ

Cecilia Metella (3, E7)
Ristorante €€€
The outside seating here is great, with glimpsed views of the jewel-green countryside around the Appia Antica from a low hill, under the shade of a rambling vine. Inside it's a bit more formal, but the

food is good and it's a fine lunch spot.
☎ 06 51 10 213 ✉ Via Appia Antica 125-127 ⏱ 12.30-3pm & 7.30-10.30pm Tue-Sun ♿ fair ♿ Ⓥ

Charly's Saucière (5, A6)
Ristorante €€€
Tucked away on the way to San Giovanni, this is Swiss-Italian, with twee lace curtains and crisp white tablecloths. For a change from pasta eat delicious Roquefort salad or different takes on steak.
☎ 06 704 95 666 ✉ Via di San Giovanni in Laterano 270 ⏱ 12.45-2.30pm & 8-11.30pm Mon-Fri, 8-11.30pm Sat Ⓜ San Giovanni ♿ Ⓥ

La Piazzetta (4, H5)
Ristorante €€
Molto simpatico and delightfully cosy, on a tiny Medieval lane, this has a fabulous antipasti buffet and equally impressive main courses, such as yolky *carbonara*. A dessert-sampler buffet means you don't have to face a difficult decision between puddings.
☎ 06 699 16 40 ✉ Vicolo del Buon Consiglio 23a ⏱ noon-3pm & 7-11pm Mon-Sat 🚌 to Via Cavour Ⓜ Cavour Ⓥ

Taverna dei Quaranta (4, J6)
Trattoria €
Off the tourist track but by the Colosseum, this high-ceilinged trattoria is run by gentle staff and offers excellent Roman dishes, with delicious daily pasta specials, great bruschetta and *arrostocini* (beef kebabs).
☎ 06 700 05 50 ✉ Via Claudia 24 ⏱ noon-3.30pm & 7.30-11.30pm Ⓜ Colosseo ♿ fair ♿ Ⓥ

TRASTEVERE

The cobbled maze of Trastevere is always abuzz, with many lovely trattorie amidst the run-of-the-mill tourist haunts.

Alle Fratte di Trastevere (2, A2)
Trattoria €€
A small, friendly trattoria with chirpy paintings, frothy curtains and outside seating: stop here for authentic food and big portions, a big hit with savvy priests, local workers and lucky tourists.
☎ 06 583 57 75 ✉ Via delle Fratte di Trastevere 49-50 ⏱ 6.30-10.45pm Thu-Tue 🚌 🚋 Viale Trastevere ♿ Ⓥ

Campo de' Fiori (p69) is the perfect spot for people-watching

Asinocotto (2, B2)
Trattoria €€€
Asinocotto is an intimate restaurant hung with grapevine lighting. Food is creative and fabulous – try the swordfish with capers and citrus fruit or a literary-referenced pud.
☎ 06 589 89 85 ✉ Via dei Vascellari 48 🕒 12.30-3pm & 7.30-11.30pm 🚃 Viale Trastevere 🚇 V

Bibli (2, A2)
Café €
A buzzing warren that manages to be a bookshop, cultural centre and café, with a little courtyard and delectable cakes. Also does *aperitivo* for peckish intelligentsia.
☎ 06 588 40 97 ✉ Via dei Fienaroli 28 🕒 usually 11am-midnight Tue-Fri, 5.30pm-midnight Mon 🚃 🚇 Viale Trastevere 🚇 V

Da Augusto (2, A2)
Trattoria €
Much-loved, well-worn Augusto would have to be one of Rome's favourite mamma's kitchens. It dishes up Roman classics such as *stracciatella* (clear broth with egg and parmesan) at traditional prices. The rickety tables spill out onto the piazza in summer.
☎ 06 580 37 98 ✉ Piazza de' Renzi 15 🕒 usually 12.30-3pm & 8-11.30pm Mon-Fri, 12.30-3pm Sat 🚃 🚇 Viale Trastevere 🚇

Da Lucia (4, D6)
Trattoria €
Eat beneath the fluttering linen and knickers of the neighbourhood at this terrific trattoria, on a narrow cobbled backstreet, which serves up a cavalcade of Roman specialities including *trippa alla romana* (tripe with tomato sauce) and *pollo con peperoni* (chicken with peppers).
☎ 06 580 36 01 ✉ Via del Mattinato 2 🕒 12.30-3.30pm & 7.30-midnight Tue-Sun 🚃 🚇 Viale Trastevere 🚇

Dar Poeta (4, D5)
Pizzeria €
A buzzing tucked-away pizzeria with a special recipe for pizzas that take the unoccupied middle ground between Roman wafers and Neopolitan comfort food. They're crispy yet a little thicker than normal, and apparently more digestible. Leave room for chocolate and ricotta calzone.
☎ 06 588 05 16 ✉ Vicolo del Bologna 45 🕒 dinner 🚇 fair 🚇 V

Ferrara (2, A2)
Ristorante €€€€
In elegant, whitewashed caverns, sophisticated Ferrara offers complex food and has the soul of an *enoteca*, with an encyclopaedic winelist. Friendly and expert waiters will guide you through, chatting about Italian wines like personal friends. Also a snug *aperitivo* stop.
☎ 06 583 339 20 ✉ Piazza Trilussa 41 🕒 8pm-1.30am Tue-Mon, *cantina* from 6pm 🚃 to Piazza Trilussa 🚇 V

LA DOLCE VITA

Rome has some delicious cake shops, concentrated around the Ghetto. Try **Bernasconi** (2, A1; Piazza B Cairoli 16), **La Dolceroma** (2, B1; Via del Portico d'Ottavia 20), or Forno del Ghetto (p70).

Forno la Renella (2, A2)
Pizza a taglio €
Some of Rome's best bread here, as well as slabs of thick, doughy pizza with simple and delicious toppings, all fired in wood-fuelled ovens. A personal favourite is potato, mozzarella and gorgonzola. Popular with everyone from old ladies with little dogs to skinheads with big dogs.
06 581 72 65 Via del Moro 15-16 9am-9pm to Piazza Trilussa V

La Botticella (4, D6)
Trattoria €€
It's worth seeking out La Botticella for a hearty welcome and vigorous versions of Roman staples such as *spaghetti all'amatriciana* and *tortino d'alici* (anchovy pie) as well as offal-based favourites that are not for the squeamish. The few outdoor tables resonate with the sounds of the neighbourhood.
06 581 47 38 Vicolo del Leopardo 39a 4pm-midnight Mon-Tue & Thu-Sat to Piazza Trilussa

La Fonte della Salute (2, A2)
Gelateria €
Perhaps not 'the fountain of health' it purports, although you can plump for soy and yogurt-based *gelati*, and the fruit flavours are so delicious that they are bound to lift your spirits. Scoops are more generous than more central places.
06 589 74 71 Via Cardinal Marmaggi 2-6 10am-1am Viale Trastevere

La Gensola (2, B2)
Trattoria €€
This Sicilian smasher fills small, brightly lit, graceful adjoining rooms, and offers really good cooking, specialising in seafood; try the delicious tuna tartare or pasta with fresh anchovies. It's unpretentious but classy and foodies will love it.
06 581 63 12
Piazza della Gensola 15
Viale Trastevere

Pizzeria al Marmi (2, A2)
Pizzeria €
Locals know it as *l'obitorio* (the morgue) because of its marble-slab tabletops, but thankfully there the similarity stops. This is one of Trastevere's liveliest pizzerias with paper-thin pizzas, no-nonsense interior, clattering atmosphere, gruff waiters and streetside seating.
06 580 09 19 Viale di Trastevere 53 7pm-2am Thu-Tue Viale Trastevere V

Pizzeria San Calisto (2, A2)
Pizzeria €
Blink and you'll miss this tiny pizzeria, which is surprisingly friendly and good value considering the busy tourist thoroughfare. There's a lengthy list of bruschetta and crostini, and more than 30 toppings for pizzas so big they hang off your plate.
06 581 82 56 Piazza di San Calisto 9a 4.30pm-midnight Tue-Sun
Viale Trastevere
V

Ripa 12 (2, A2)
Calabrian €€€
A family-run Calabrian seafood joint, cosy, with a wooden ceiling and what look like grandma's dining-room chairs, this place cooks the freshest fish with a sophisticated menu that belies the plain interior – *carpaccio di spigola* (very fine slices of raw sea bass) was possibly invented here.
06 580 90 93 Via di San Francesco a Ripa 12 noon-3pm & 7.30pm-midnight Mon-Sat
Viale Trastevere

Da Sergio (p69) – don't let the clown scare you off

Sora Lella (2, B2)
Trattoria €€€€
On tiny Tiber island, you ring the doorbell to gain entrance to this timeless Roman institution. The classic Roman menu has some culinary twists as well as crowd-pleasers like *amatriciana* with gnocchi (perfect for a winter's night).
☎ 06 686 16 01 ✉ Via Ponte Quattro Capi 16 ⏲ 1-2.30pm & 8-11pm Mon-Sat 🚌 🚊 Viale Trastevere

AROUND THE VATICAN

Watch out near St Peter's for overpriced, underwhelming tourist cafés; amid the trash there are various good restaurants and cafés in this sedate, stately district. See p64 for a few more.

Osteria dell'Angelo (4, B1)
Trattoria €€
Boxing and rugby dominate at this hugely popular neighbourhood trattoria a few minutes from the Vatican. It's plastered with memorabilia of the owner's sporting heroes and offers solid wooden furniture, a sociable atmosphere and robust versions of Roman favourites like *tonnarelli cacio e pepe* and scrumptious meatballs.
☎ 06 372 94 70 ✉ Via Giovanni Bettolo 24 ⏲ 12.30-2.30pm & 8-11pm Mon-Sat Ⓜ Ottaviano 🚻 Ⓥ

FOOD WITH A VIEW

To overlook dazzling Piazza del Popolo try unfailingly trendy Dal Bolognese (p75), while you can eat overlooking lovely Piazza Farnese at traditional Ar Galletto (p69). For sweeping views, there's the hidden terrace café (p70) at the Capitoline Museums or greenery-draped Ciampini al Caffè du Jardin (p74). To overlook the Spanish Steps head to sun-trap Il Palazzetto (p75). The view from the café on the ramparts of Castel Sant'Angelo (p27) – where Tosca threw herself off (but not because of the coffee) – is also splendid, and from Cecilia Metella (p77) on Appia Antica you glimpse lush, green countryside a world away from central Rome.

Siciliainbocca (3, A3)
Sicilian €€
Splendidly sunny (in demeanor and décor), this is a great place to sample Sicilian specialities like *caponata* (browned vegetables, anchovies and capers) and desserts like *cannoli* (fried pastry tubes) accompanied by *pantelleria*, the island's ridiculously good moscato.
☎ 06 373 58 400 ✉ Via Faa di Bruno 26 ⏲ 1-3pm & 8-11.30pm Mon-Sat Ⓜ Ottaviano 🚻 Ⓥ

Living *la dolce vita* in Piazza Navona (p71)

AROUND PIAZZA BARBERINI

The busy area around Piazza Barberini – near the Fontana di Trevi – contains some good finds and possibly Rome's best ice cream.

Colline Emiliane (4, H3)
Emilia-Romagna €€
Emilia-Romagna gave the world parmesan, balsamic vinegar and Parma ham, and as you might expect, this serene culinary outpost is exceptionally good: try delicious *tortelli di zucca* (pumpkin pasta) and *gimabonnetto* (roast veal with roast potatoes).
☎ 06 481 75 38 ⊠ Via degli Avignonesi 22 ⏰ 12.45-2.45pm & 7.45-10.45pm Sat-Thu Ⓜ Barberini ♿

Da Ricci (4, J4)
Pizzeria €
Possibly Rome's oldest pizzeria, Est! Est! Est! (as it is also known) began life as a wine shop in 1905 and is still run by the same family. Nowadays it offers deep-crust *pizza alla napoletana* in a bygone atmosphere, doing a busy, boisterous trade.
☎ 06 488 11 07 ⊠ Via Genova 32 ⏰ 7.30-11.30pm Tue-Sun 🚌 to Via Nazionale Ⓜ Repubblica ♿ Ⓥ

Il Chianti (4, G3)
Ristorante-Enoteca €
Ideal if you're feeling peckish around the Fontana di Trevi, this is a gem amid the tourist dross, a perfectly good restaurant specialising in Tuscan dishes, also serving pizza, and home-made foccacia. You can equally stop

A salad of marinated tuna belly, black olives and fennel

for a contemplative glass of wine.
☎ 06 678 75 50 ⊠ Via del Lavatore 81-82a ⏰ 12.30-3.30pm & 7-11.30pm Mon-Sat Ⓜ Barberini ♿ good ♿ Ⓥ

Papa Baccus (4, H1)
Tuscan €€€
Using authentic Tuscan ingredients, smart Papa Baccus takes good food seriously and proffers delicious rural specialities, with Chianina beef and *spalla di Cinta* (shoulder Sienese pork) among the highlights. There's plenty besides, including *panzanella* (a delicious, summery starter of bread with salad, herbs and oil).
☎ 06 427 42 808 🖥 www .papabaccus.com ⊠ Via Toscana 36 ⏰ 12.30-3pm & 7.30-11pm Mon-Fri, 7.30-11pm Sat 🚌 to Via Veneto Ⓥ

San Crispino (4, G3)
Gelataria €
Most agree that San Crispino, with its natural seasonal flavours, is Rome's best ice cream, and we're willing to stake a whole tub of wild orange on it. As befits such culinary heights, atmosphere

is a bit hoity toity and servings a bit small.
☎ 06 679 39 24 ⊠ Via della Panetteria 42 ⏰ noon-12.30am Mon, Wed, Thu & Sun, to 1.30am Fri & Sat ♿ Ⓥ

AROUND TERMINI

Termini's surrounds are Rome's most multicultural zone and have the city's best ethnic eats. Further east, San Lorenzo, the university district, offers lots of attitude and some sophisticated finds.

Africa (5, B2)
Ethiopian & Eritrean €
Deep-striped Africa really feels like you could be somewhere else, catering to local expats and curious Romans. Dig into spicy snacks such as falafel and *sambusas* (a cross between a spring roll and a samosa) and scoop up meat and vegetables with soft, spongy *injera* bread. Top it off with sweet halva and spicy tea.
☎ 06 494 10 77 ⊠ Via Gaeta 26-8 ⏰ noon-4pm & 8pm-midnight Tue-Sun 🚌 to Piazza dell'Independenza Ⓜ Castro Pretorio ♿ Ⓥ

Agata e Romeo (5, B4)
Ristorante €€€€
Here Agata's marvellous culinary innovations co-star husband Romeo's veritable wine cellar. Menus pay homage to Roman tradition as well as providing creative delicacies; don't miss Agata's legendary *millefoglie* (puff pastry with custard). Attention to detail and fine dining are paramount, décor is a refined buttercup-yellow.
☎ 06 446 61 15 ✉ Via Carlo Alberto 45 ✆ 1-3pm & 7.30-11pm Mon-Fri Ⓜ Vittorio E

Al Forno della Soffitta (5, A1)
Pizzeria €
None of those namby-pamby thin-crusts here, this cheerful, busy, brightly decorated place is authentic Neapolitan-style, with substantial dough and plentiful, delicious toppings (dig in and share a pizza with a selection of different flavours).
☎ 06 420 11 164 ✉ Via Piave 62-64 ✆ 12.30-3pm & 7.30pm-midnight Mon-Fri, 7.30pm-midnight Sat & Sun ♿ Ⓥ

Snacks at the Spanish Steps

Olives to tempt any tastebud

Formula 1 (3, E4)
Pizzeria €
The name reflects the whistle-stop style of this historic joint, perennially packed with students and slumming uptowners. Join the pushy queue and be assertive. Placemats double as menus – order tasty snacks like bruschetta and stuffed zucchini flowers as well as classic thin-crusts from whizzing-by waiters.
☎ 06 445 38 66 ✉ Via degli Equi 13, San Lorenzo ✆ 6.30pm-1.30am Mon-Sat 🚍 to Via Tiburtina ♿ Ⓥ

Hang Zhou (5, A4)
Chinese €
Endearing and hugely popular, this has a mainland China vibe, plastered with Chairman Mao kitsch and proprietor Sonia pictured with famous and not-in-the-least-famous clientele. The food's reasonably good, if catering for Western tastes: recommended are dumplings and black rice.
☎ 06 487 27 32 ✉ Via San Martino ai Monti ✆ noon-3pm & 7-11.30pm Ⓜ Vittorio Emanuelle ♿ Ⓥ

Indian Fast Food (5, B4)
Indian €
Under glaring neon, this is a splendid Indian takeaway, with great, authentic curries and spicy samosas – just point at what you want. You can also eat in, inspired by Hindi hits.
☎ 06 446 07 92 ✉ Via Mamiani 11 ✆ 11am-4pm & 5-10.30pm Ⓜ Vittorio Emanuele ♿ Ⓥ

Trattoria Monti (5, A4)
Le Marche €€€
The Camerucci family run this inviting, intimate cave-like trattoria, offering traditional cooking from the Marches region on the Adriatic coast. Expect homemade soups, gamey stews, elaborate pasta combinations and ingredients such as *pecorino di fossa* (ewe's milk aged in caves), *funghi* and truffles. Book ahead.
☎ 06 446 65 73 ✉ Via di San Vito 13a ✆ 1-2.45pm & 8-10.45pm Tue-Sat, 1-2.45pm Sun Ⓜ Vittorio Emanuele Ⓥ

Uno e Bino (3, E4)
Ristorante €€€
An intimate, sophisticated award-winner, Uno e Bino stands out from San Lorenzo's mostly student oriented venues. Classy yet relaxed, it's simply decorated to better concentrate on the fine, adventurous food. It has

won lots of awards and you'll need to book.

☎ 06 446 07 02 ✉ Via degli Equi 58, San Lorenzo ⏰ Tue-Sun 🚍 to Via Tiburtina Ⓥ

TESTACCIO & OSTIENSE

Testaccio, near the former abattoir, offers traditional *cucina romana* – with a prevalence of the fifth quarter (offal).

Agustarello (2, A4)
Trattoria €€
Old-timer Agustarello hides its in-the-know hubbub behind frosted glass. Inside it's thoroughly Roman, from the clientele to the food. Near the site of the city's former abattoir, it specialises in making the most of tripe, oxtail, and other bits, so avoid if you think offal is awful.

☎ 06 574 65 85 ✉ Via Giovanni Branca 98 ⏰ 12.30-3.30pm & 7.30pm-midnight Mon-Sat 🚍 to Via Marmorata ♿

Checchino dal 1887 (2, B5)
Ristorante €€€
In a graceful whitewashed arched room, with chandeliers and smart waiters, this is

Testaccio's most sophisticated take on the *quinto quarto*, going strong since the 19th century. Specialities include *rigatoni con pajata* (pasta with veal intestines) and *coda alla vaccinara* (braised oxtail) although there are other dishes if those bits don't tickle your fancy.

☎ 06 574 38 16 ✉ Via di Monte Testaccio 30 ⏰ 12.30-3pm & 8pm-midnight Tue-Sun 🚍 to Via Marmorata Ⓥ

Da Felice (2, B5)
Trattoria €
Film director Benigni has written a poem to this place. The food is great and cheap (try the tender *saltimbocca* – 'leap in the mouth' – veal wrapped in prosciutto), and there's the added thrill of getting in – it's full if you don't cut it with the famously grumpy proprietor. Don your Roma colours or practise your Roman accent.

☎ 06 574 68 00 ✉ Via Mastro Giorgio 29 ⏰ 12.30-3pm & 8-10.30pm Mon-Sat 🚍 to Via Marmorata ♿

Hostaria da Enzo (2, C6)
Trattoria €
With just a few tables, this is a classic Roman family

trattoria that's been here for around 50 years. Used to feeding up the workers from the nearby market, the cook formerly fed members of parliament. The fresh pasta dishes are delicious, sausages super and the tiramisu feathery light.

☎ 06 574 13 64 ✉ Via Ostiense 36 ⏰ Mon-Sat Ⓜ Pyramide ♿ Ⓥ

Remo (2, B4)
Pizzeria €
Here, queuing is all part of the experience (get here early or late to avoid a long wait). When you eventually win that crammed-in table amid the noisy happy hoards, you're given a pen and pre-printed list for ordering. Pizzas are paper thin and sizzling with toppings; burly pizza-makers look like they may have done more.

☎ 06 574 62 70 ✉ Piazza Santa Maria Liberatrice 44 ⏰ 7.30pm-1am Mon-Sat 🚍 to Via Marmorata ♿ Ⓥ

Trattoria de Bucatino (2, B4)
Trattoria €€
You might have trouble finding a table at this intimate, convivial, high-ceilinged place (seating indoor and out). Food is splendid, offering huge portions of traditional dishes such as *bucatini all'amatriciana*, as well as great pizza. *Secondi* are equally good and dolci delectable.

☎ 06 574 68 86 ✉ Via Luca della Robbia 84 ⏰ 12.30-3pm & 7.30-11.30pm Tue-Sun 🚍 Via Marmorata ♿ fair ♿ Ⓥ

Sandwiches – Italian style

Entertainment

Romans are renowned for knowing how to enjoy life. Ambling around on a balmy evening checking out everyone else doing the same is a favoured activity, but there are many more structured things to do, whether it's opera or football, orchestra or jazz, dance or drinking.

There are year-round festivals, but Rome is most vibrant in summer, when many performances of dance, music, opera and theatre take place under the stars, in parks, gardens and church courtyards, and clubs move outside onto terraces and beaches. Stalls, bars and entertainments sprout around Isola Tiberina and outdoor cinemas are set up on the island and in Piazza Vittorio Emanuele.

The *centro storico* (historic city centre) gets busy after dark. Campo de' Fiori is popular with a young crowd, the alleyways around Piazza Navona have some trendy late-night hangouts and just about everyone descends on Trastevere to stroll and stop at its friendly bars. However, most clubs are based around Testaccio and Ostiense, south of Trastevere. Testaccio has a unique area devoted solely to clubs and bars, circling a small hummock created

FESTIVAL HOTLINES

It's hard to keep track of all Rome's festivals. Venues vary – check listings or contact the organisers.

Concerti a Villa Giulia (☎ 06 808 20 58)

Cosmophonies (www.cosmophonies .com)

Estate Romana (www.estateromana .it)

Invito alla Danza (☎ 06 442 92 323; www.invitoalladanza.it)

Isola del Cinema (☎ 06 583 31 13; www.isoladelcinema.com)

New Operafestival (☎ 06 561 15 19; www.newoperafestivaldiroma.com)

Notte Bianca (☎ 06 06 06; www .lanottebianca.it)

Notti di Cinema a Piazza Vittorio (☎ 06 443 61 107; www.agisanec .lazio.it)

Roma Incontra il Mondo (☎ 06 418 03 69; www.villaada.org)

Roma Jazz Festival (☎ 06 563 05 015; www.romajazzfestival.it)

Romaeuropa Festival (☎ 800 795 525; www.romaeuropa.net)

Teatro dell'Opera Summer Season (☎ 06 808 83 52; www.opera.roma.it)

Villa Celimontana Jazz (☎ 199 10 97 83, box office 06 77 20 84; www .villacelimontanajazz.com)

from ancient discarded pottery – Monte di Testaccio. Other clubs are dotted further out into the suburbs. There is also an alternative 'social centre' scene – squatter arts venues that provide the city's counterculture (see p93), featuring frequent DJs, cutting-edge bands, contemporary art and political events. As you look uncool when you're drunk, and drinks are often expensive, overt drunkenness is rarely seen.

What's On

For most comprehensive entertainment listings, check *Roma C'è* – there's a small English section at the back – published on Thursdays and available from newsstands. *Wanted in Rome*, published on alternate Wednesdays, contains listings and reviews. The daily newspapers *Il Messaggero* and *La Repubblica* list theatre, cinema and special events.

SPECIAL EVENTS

January/February
Carnevale Children wear fancy dress.

March/April
Festa della Primavera The Spanish Steps are filled with azaleas.

April
Natale di Roma 21 April; Rome's birthday (she was a sprightly 2758 in 2005). Bands perform in Piazza del Campidoglio.

May
International Literature Festival Readings by literary hardhitters in the Basilica di Massenzio until June.
Primo Maggio 1 May; Labour Day pop-concert extravaganza in San Giovanni.
Via dei Coronari Mostra-Mercato Antiques fair.

June
Accademia Nazionale di Santa Cecilia Concert series at Villa Giulia.
Cosmphonies Until July; season of theatre, music and dance at Ostia Antica.
Estate Romana Until September; hundreds of events, supported and promoted by the city authorities.
New Operafestival Opera in San Clemente's Renaissance courtyard until July.
Roma Incontra il Mondo World music festival in Villa Ada grounds next to a small lake, from June to August.
San Pietro e San Paolo 29 June; public holiday, celebrations and processions for Rome's patron saints Peter and Paul.
Teatro dell'Opera di Roma Summer season at Terme di Caracalla till mid-August.
Villa Celimontana Jazz Until September; atmospheric jazz festival, under the stars.

July
Festa di Noantri Trastevere's residents celebrate over local wine and *porchetta* (ham roasted with herbs).
Invito alla Danza Contemporary and classical dance at Villa Massimo.
Isola del Cinema Until mid-August; international film festival.
OperaEstate Opera concerts and recitals in at Sant'Ivo alla Sapienza.

August
Notti di Cinema a Piazza Vittorio Until early September; open-air cinema in the most multicultural part of town.

September
La Notte Bianca Galleries, museums and shops open and free concerts and performances 8pm to 8am.
Venezia a Roma Venice Film Festival movies get a quick pre-release showing.
Via dell'Orso Craft Fair Open studios, torchlit in the evening.

October/November
Roma Jazz Festival Top performers do their thing, with concerts at Parco della Musica and La Palma.
Romaeuropa Festival Edgy theatre, dance and opera performances at Parco della Musica and Teatro Valle.
Via dei Coronari Mostra-Mercato Antiques fair.

December
Piazza Navona Christmas Fair 1 December to 6 January; market stalls sell Christmassy stuff, crib figures and kitsch souvenirs.
Presepi time Churches around Rome set up their nativity scenes.

CLASSICAL MUSIC & OPERA

Accademia Filarmonica Romana (3, B2)

Founded in 1821, Rome's music academy alumni number Rossini, Donizetti and Verdi. The programme (October to May) features mainly chamber and choral music, with some contemporary concerts, opera, and ballet.

☎ 06 320 17 52 ⌨ www
.filarmonicaromana.org, Italian only ✉ Teatro Olimpico, Piazza Gentile da Fabriano 17 € €15-30 ⏲ varies
🚌 🚈 to Piazza Manzini

Accademia Nazionale di Santa Cecilia (3, B1)

Under the direction of Italian-American conductor Antonio Pappano, this prestigious academy presents programmes devoted to single composers or themes in its spectacular new home, the Parco della Musica. Guesting are the world's greatest conductors and soloists.

☎ 06 32 81 71 ⌨ www
.santacecilia.it ✉ Viale Pietro de Coubertin 30 € varies ⏲ varies 🚌 to Via Flaminia

Auditorium Parco della Musica (3, B1)

Rome's new €140 million, Renzo Piano–designed venue has three theatres resembling futuristic turtles around an open-air arena and hosts classical, opera, pop, theatre and ballet. The 2756-seater Sala Santa Cecilia is Europe's largest concert hall, with a billowing-wood ceiling and marvellous acoustics.

☎ 06 802 41 281 ⌨ www
.auditorium.com ✉ Viale Pietro de Coubertin 30

€ €9/5-7 ⏲ 1hr guided visits hourly 10.30am-4.30pm Sat-Sun; performances vary
🚌 to Via Flaminia

Istituzione Universitaria dei Concerti (3, D4)

The recitals and chamber-music concerts held in the Aula Magna of La Sapienza university range from classical to contemporary: it could be Mozart one week and the Steve Martland band the next.

☎ 06 361 00 51 ⌨ www
.concertiiuc.it, Italian only ✉ Piazzale Aldo Moro 5 € 10-15 ⏲ varies 🚌 492 Ⓜ Castro Pretorio

Teatro dell'Opera di Roma (5, A3)

The fascist-era exterior of Rome's opera house is a plain-clothes disguise for the 19th-century gilt-and-cherubs interior that has hosted many greats, among them the premiere of Giacomo Puccini's *Tosca*. Despite a reputation as the poor cousin of Milan's La Scala, it's still well worth a visit. In summer it moves to the Baths of Caracalla.

☎ 06 481 70 03, booking 800 90 70 80 ⌨ www
.opera.roma.it ✉ Piazza Beniamino Gigli 8 € approx €9-130 ⏲ varies; season Dec-Jun Ⓜ Repubblica

Teatro Ghione (4, B4)

A former cinema, this is now an exquisitely decorated theatre near St Peter's, often featuring wonderful events, with an eclectic programme of recitals, often featuring international opera legends.

☎ 06 637 22 94 ⌨ www
.ghione.it, Italian only ✉ Via delle Fornaci 37 € 10-15 ⏲ varies 🚌 62

THEATRE & DANCE

Rome has a thriving theatre scene, though you'll have to understand Italian to get the most out of it. However, there are regular productions in English too. Look out in local listings for current offerings, or the **English Theatre of Rome** (☎ 06 687 94 19; www.romethe atre.com) performs well-received productions in English from October to June, and every summer the **Miracle Players** (☎ 06 703 93 427; www.miracleplayers .com) puts on plays in English in the Roman Forum. Rome is also a regular stop on international dance company itineraries.

Many venues are worth visiting for the architecture and decoration as well as for what's going on inside.

Teatro Argentina (6, C4)

This opened in 1792 and preserves its garlanded frescoed ceiling which surmounts layer upon layer of red-curtained boxes. Rossini's *Barber of Seville* premiered here and it's still home to fine theatre and

Ideal for the culture vulture – Teatro Argentina

dance. It's the official home of the Teatro di Roma. Book early for the dance productions.
☎ 06 637 22 94
🖥 www.teatrodiroma.net
✉ Largo di Torre Argentina 42 € €10-26 🕙 varies
🚌 🚊 to Largo Argentina

Teatro Olimpico (3, B2)
In the northern suburbs, Rome's leading dance stage often hosts world-class dance troupes, ranging from classical to avant-garde. Momix, New York City Ballet, Jiri Kylian and Lindsay Kemp have all performed in recent years.
☎ 06 326 59 91 🖥 www .teatroolimpico.it ✉ Piazza Gentile da Fabriano 17
€ from €15 🕙 varies
🚊 2 to Piazza Mancini

Teatro Silvano Toti Globe (3, C3)
This replica of Shakespeare's Globe matches London's, open to the elements, with capacity for 1250, 420 standing. Expect a rich season of the bard's works – and it's less likely to rain than London too.
☎ 06 820 77 304 🖥 www .globetheatreroma.com
✉ Villa Borghese, entrance

from Largo Aqua Felix
€ €7-18 🕙 box office 1-9.15pm Thu-Sun Jun-Sep
🚻 excellent 🚹

Teatro Valle (6, C3)
Perfectly proportioned Teatro Valle is like a mini opera house, with three levels of private boxes. The programme offers music from recitals to torch songs and occasionally includes subtitled works.
☎ 06 688 03 794 🖥 www .teatrovalle.it ✉ Via del Teatro Valle 23a € varies

🕙 varies 🚌 🚊 to Largo Argentina

Teatro Vascello (3, A5)
This cutting-edge contemporary theatre nestles in the bosom of leafy Monteverdo. This is a striking space for the latest fringe works with lots of multi-media and cross-cultural nuggets alongside new takes on classics.
☎ 06 588 10 21 🖥 www .teatrovascello.it ✉ Via Carina 72 € varies
🕙 varies 🚌 Via Carini

CINEMA

Cinema is popular in Rome and there are plenty of movie theatres. Films are usually dubbed into Italian; those screened in the original language (with Italian subtitles) are indicated in listings by *versione originale* (VO) or *'in Inglese'* (in English). They're shown regularly at **Metropolitan Multisala** (4, F1; ☎ 06 326 005 00; www .medusacinema.it; Via del Corso 7) and **Warner Village Cinemas Moderno** (5, A3; ☎ 06 477 779 11; www .warnervillage.net; Piazza della Repubblica). Tickets usually cost €7/4.

Outdoor cinema is all the rage during the summer: see Special Events (p85) and Festival Hotlines (p84) for details.

For listings check *Roma C'e, La Republica* or try www .capital.it/trovacinema.

BARS & PUBS

Rome offers three drinking options: bars/cafés (where all ages are welcome), wine bars (*enoteche*) or pubs (*birrerie*).

Bar San Calisto (2, A2)

This is a rough-and-ready café-bar – precisely its charm in boho Trastevere. Shady characters hang around outside, and doughty elderly ladies and gents hog the inner tables. The soft, creamy chocolate *gelato* is a contender for best in town.
☎ 06 583 58 69
✉ Piazza San Calisto 4
🕐 6am-1.30am Mon-Sat
🚌 🚊 Viale Trastevere 🚻

Relax at Bar del Fico

Bar del Fico (6, A1)

Convivial and cosy, with outside tables filling a fig tree–shaded piazza, this wonderfully relaxed spot is buzzing and friendly, popular with local actors, artists, students and chess-playing old timers.
☎ 06 686 52 05 ✉ Piazza del Fico 26 🕐 8am-2am Mon-Sat, 6pm-2am Sun
🚌 to Corso Rinascimento

Bar della Pace (6, A1)

Fronted by a flood of ivy, gilt-mirrored, wood-panelled Bar della Pace is both trendy and touristy, and ideal for an early-evening summer apéritif outside as it is for a leisurely winter nightcap. Great for watching the world go by.
☎ 06 686 12 16 ✉ Via della Pace 5 🕐 9am-3am
🚌 to Corso Rinascimento

Baronato Quattro Bellezze (4, D3)

A charmingly theatrical, tiny bar, with a rocking horse wrapped in fairy lights suspended above the bar. On Thursdays, Tunisian drag queen owner Dominot dons wig and gown and performs Piaf songs. Reserve a table for the Piaf show.
☎ 06 687 28 65 ✉ Via di Panico 23 🕐 7pm-3am Tue-Sun 🚌 to Corso Vittorio Emanuele II

Bohemien (4, H5)

This is a cosy little artsy café-winery, with mismatched tables and booklined walls, aptly named for its boho crowd. A great place for a quiet drink or a cup of tea and slice of cake.
✉ Via degli Zingari 36 🕐 10am-2pm & 5pm-2am Tue-Sun Ⓜ Cavour

Trendy Bar della Pace

Crudo (2, A1)

With flickering light projections and paint-streaked walls, this lounge bar-restaurant is almost too cool for school. And that goes for the patrons and the food, because everything served here is raw. Warm up with a cocktail. There's an intimate restaurant upstairs.
☎ 06 683 89 89 ✉ Via degli Specchi 6 🕐 6pm-2.30am Tue-Sun 🚌 Via Arenula Ⓥ 🚻

Fiddler's Elbow (5, A4)

This was Italy's first Irish pub (opened in 1976). A small doorway leads to a delightfully dishevelled, cosy and warrenlike interior, with rickety wooden benches,

---

TIME FOR WINE

At *enoteche* (wine bars) you can drink *and* eat, so several are listed in Eating rather than here. However you can just as well drop by to drink. Lovely places to get stuck into wines include: L'Angelo Divino (2, A1; p69), Casa Bleve (6, C3; p71), Enoteca Corsi (6, D3; p71), Cul de Sac (6, A2; p71), Antica Enoteca (4, F2; p74), 'Gusto (4, F2; p75), Palatium (4, F2; p76), Il Palazzetto (4, G2; p75), Ferrara (2, A2; p78), and Il Chianti (4, G3; p81).

friendly staff and Italian and foreign clientele, and decent pints of Guinness.

☎ 06 487 21 10 ✉ Via dell'Olmata 43 ⌚ 4.30pm-12.30am Ⓜ Cavour

Freni e Frizioni (2, A2)

A hip, laidback booklined haunt (in a former garage, hence the name, brakes and clutches) hung with cool modern art, this has tasty, cheap *aperitivo* (€5) and easy-on-the-eye clientele spilling into the small piazza.

☎ 06 583 342 10 ✉ Via del Politeanna 4-6 ⌚ 10am-2am 🚌 to Viale di Trastevere

Il Giardino dei Cilegi (2, A2)

A gay-owned, sepia-toned tearoom, this has seating on white banquettes with small wooden tables, wiggly twigs and tiny touches of baroque, under a ceiling of softly lit autumn leaves. Good for cakes, cocktails and *aperitivo*.

☎ 06 580 34 23 ✉ Via dei Fienaroli 4 ⌚ 5pm-12.30am Mon-Sat, 1pm-12.30am Sun 🚌 Ⓥ Viale Trastevere ♿ Ⓥ

Bend your arm at Fiddler's

Lose a few hours with a cocktail or two at Ombre Rosse

La Vineria (6, A4)

The best bar on Campo de' Fiori, where locals and tourists crush and mingle. There's a range of inexpensive beers and wines, the staff are funky and friendly and the outside tables are the most coveted on the campo.

☎ 06 688 03 268 ✉ Campo de' Fiori ⌚ 7.30am-2am 🚌 to Corso Vittorio Emanuele II

L'Oasi della Birra (2, B4)

The oasis of beer is just that, plus an upmarket deli and winery thrown in. Sit downstairs in the cosy woodlined cavelike basement and indulge in an obscure beer, while tucking into tasty cold cuts.

☎ 06 574 61 22 ✉ Piazza Testaccio 41 ⌚ 7.30am-12.30am Mon-Sat 🚌 Via Marmorata ♿ Ⓥ

Modo (6, A1)

A new black-and-white confection – consider wearing black to fit in. It's a designer bar with a difference: live music nightly at 11pm (usually the Rome hot favourite: jazz), followed by DJs.

☎ 06 686 74 52 🖥 www.modaroma.it ✉ Vicolo del Fico 3 ⌚ 7.30pm-2am 🚌 to Corso Vittorio Emanuelle II

Ombre Rosse (4, D6)

A popular Trastevere hub that's perfect for watching the human traffic, this café-bar is a cosy spot to while away a few hours sipping cocktails and keeping an eye out for a much-coveted outside table.

☎ 06 58 84 155 ✉ Piazza Sant'Egidio 12 ⌚ 8am-2am Mon-Sat, from 6pm Sun 🚌 to Piazza Trilussa

Opera (4, D5)

This arty two-floor café-bar has changing exhibitions and is a friendly, shoebox-sized Trastevere pitstop. The *aperitivo* is excellent, and there's a great weekend brunch (€15); an ideal hangover cure.

☎ 06 583 356 97 🖥 www.operarome.com ✉ Via della Scala 43 ⌚ 4pm-2am Tue-Sat, 11am-2am Sun 🚌 to Viale di Trastevere

Salotto 42 (6, D1)

Run by a Swedish-Italian couple, Salotto's glass front faces the incredible Temple of Apollo. Inside is smart but informal and cosy, with a selection of books, a snaking 19th-century Murano glass chandelier, and chic seating to sink into.

☎ 06 678 58 04 ✉ Piazza di Pietra 42 ⌚ 10.30am-2am Tue-Sun 🚌 to Via del Corso

ROME IN FILM

Rome has starred in many a feature, including *Caro Diario*, Fellini's *La Dolce Vita* (which starred Marcello Mastroianni, left, and launched him into fame and fortune) and *Roma, Ladri di Biciclette, Roma Città Aperta, Roman Holiday, The Talented Mr Ripley, Three Coins in the Fountain, The Belly of an Architect, Ocean's 12* and *Mission Impossible III*.

Ben Hur, *Cleopatra* and *Spartacus* were all filmed at local Cinecittà film studio, and Spaghetti Westerns kept it going through the early '60s. It has regained its status in recent years, hosting production for Roberto Begnini's *Life is Beautiful*, Martin Scorcese's *Gangs of New York* and Mel Gibson's *The Passion* amid much TV trash.

Société Lutèce (6, A1)
A cool bar that attracts cool people, enough of them to fill the entire street outside. Here you'll hear good (house with quirky bass lines) music and can check out lots of people just as cute as yourself (think art-school dishevelled chic and great bone structure).
☎ 06 68 30 14 72 ✉ Piazza Monte Vecchio ☽ 7pm-2am ▣ to Corso Vittorio Emanuele II

Stardust (2, A2)
This shotglass-sized char-ismatic Trastevere haunt is just the place for an intimate tête-à-tête. It's mellow in the early evenings and positively purring late-night when crowds pile in and grizzly, sexy jazz sets the tone.
☎ 06 583 20 875 ✉ Vicolo dei Renzi 4 ☽ 4pm-2am Mon-Sat, noon-2am Sun ▣ to Viale di Trastevere

Supperclub (6, C3)
Is it a bar? Is it a restaurant? Is it a cabaret joint? No, it's the Supperclub! An enter-tainment bonanza (sister to the Amsterdam version) for Rome's beautiful people. Re-cline on white divans, eat a violin-serenaded dinner, then strut your designer-dressed stuff in the disco.
☎ 06 688 072 07 ✉ Via de' Nari 14 ☽ 8pm-2am Mon-Sat ▣ to Largo Argentina

Trinity College (6, E2)
The imported beers, great food and an easy-going ambience pull in the crowds to this cheery Roman Irish pub stalwart. It gets packed to overflowing weekends – get there early to get in.
☎ 06 678 64 72 ✉ Via del Collegio Romano 6 ☽ 11am-3am ▣ to Via del Corso

Zest (5, C4)
A glamorous, minimalist, nouveau-chic hotel bar that's ideal for living it up like a bright young thing by supping a few quiet cocktails (it's rarely busy). Big plate-glass windows open onto a luminously lit poolside terrace.
☎ 06 444 841 ✉ Via Filippo Turati 171 ☽ 6.30pm-1am Ⓜ Termini

CLUBS & LIVE GIGS

Although there are clubs scattered across the centre and the suburbs, Roman clubland is concentrated in ex-industrial Testaccio and Ostiense.

Nightlife all starts slowly: Romans hit the tiles after 1am. Fridays and Saturdays are the biggest club nights, with Saturday attracting lots of dressed-up suburban kids. Many venues charge admission, which can stretch to €20 (often includ-ing the first drink).

At many clubs you have to dress up to get past the heavies at the velvet rope, though at social centres (see the boxed text, p93) dressing down is the look of choice.

In the sticky heat of July and August many clubs shut up shop and set up outdoor alternatives – many along the beaches (weekends) out of town at Fregene and Ostia, 25km south of the city.

Alexanderplatz (4, A1)

Rome loves jazz, and this is its finest jazz and blues haunt, with regular international stars. You'll need to book if you want dinner, while music starts around 10.30pm. July to September, the club moves outside to Villa Celiamontana (see p85).
☎ 06 397 42 171 🖳 www
.alexanderplatz.it ✉ Via
Ostia 9 € admission
with membership €7
⏰ 9pm-2am Mon-Sat
Ⓜ Ottaviano

Alien (3, D3)

Flat maxi-screens, black leather sofas, industrial steel and sexy little things sipping long drinks are the distinctive features of this Alien, with mainstream club fare (familiar house, techno and hip hop). Dress to impress and expect a young crowd.
☎ 06 841 22 12 🖳 www
.aliendisco.it ✉ Via Velletri
13 € €15-20 ⏰ 10.30pm-
4am Tue-Sat 🚌 38, 313

Big Mama (2, A3)

To wallow in the Eternal City blues, there's no better than this cramped Trastevere basement, which hosts well-known Italian and international names. You can reserve a table by calling or going online.
☎ 06 581 25 51 🖳 www
.bigmama.it ✉ Via di
San Francesco a Ripa 18
€ monthly/annual membership €8/12, occasionally admission charges ⏰ 9pm-
1.30am 🚌 🚋 Viale di
Trastevere

Black Out Rock Club
(3, D6)

For those about to rock, we salute you: Black Out has been ploughing an alternative furrow since 1979 and serves up a Molotov cocktail of punk, rock, ska and indie sounds, with occasional live bands.
☎ 06 704 96 791 🖳 www
.blackoutrock club.com
✉ Via Saturnia 18
€ around €8 ⏰ 10pm-

4am Fri & Sat, closed Jul & Aug Ⓜ San Giovanni

Brancaleone (3, F1)

Though north of the city, this cutting-edge, stylish social centre is worth the journey if there's a good night – top DJs play here. Friday nights (techno, drum 'n' bass) are most popular. It attracts mostly under 25s.
☎ 06 82 00 09 59 🖳 www
.brancaleone.it ✉ Via
Levanna 11 € from €5
⏰ 10.30pm-5am Thu-Sun
🚌 to Monte Sacro

Café Latino (2, B5)

A bubbly disco with a breezy terrace along the Monte Testaccio strip, here you can enjoy ethnic eclectica and dazzle with your Latino and Samba shimmies to the nightly live acts. Pure pop sometimes gets a look in.
☎ 06 572 88 556 ✉ Via di
Monte Testaccio 96 € to €15
⏰ 10.30pm-3am Thu-Sat
Ⓜ Pyramid

Kick back with some very cool blues and jazz at Alexanderplatz

Casa del Jazz (3, C6)

In a large southern park, this three-floor villa once belonged to a mafia boss – when he was caught the Comune di Roma converted it into the splendid House of Jazz, with a 150-seat auditorium and regular classy jazz gigs.
☎ 06 489 41 208 ☐ www .casajazz.it ✉ Viale di Porta Ardeatina 55 € varies ☽ 7.30pm-1am ☒ to Via Cristoforo Colombo

Circolo degli Artisti (3, E5)

The laid-back Artist's Circle club is always fun, with '80s night Screamadelica on Saturday, hip hop and electronica on Wednesday and gay night on Friday. Also a top alternative venue for live bands.
☎ 06 703 05 684 ☐ www .circoloartisti.it ✉ Via Casilina Vecchia 42 € varies ☽ varies ☒ to Via Casilina

Classico Village (3,C7)

Check out what's on and pay a visit to this eclectic venue in a made-over former factory, with several performance spaces (with frequent live jazz) around a pretty court-

Rome gets its fair share of concerts

yard. Happening designer-disco So is part of the complex if you want a change of tempo – it's packed with beautiful people and offers buzzing basslines.
☎ 06 574 33 64 ☐ www .classico.it ✉ Via Giuseppe Libetta 3 € varies ☽ varies Ⓜ Garbatella

Ex Magazzini (2, B6)

Not as maximo trendy as it was, but still a nightlife force to be reckoned with (it's been bumping-and-grinding for over 10 years), this is a converted warehouse on two floors attracting a dressed-up crowd. Expect queues and occasional live performances.
☎ 06 575 80 40 ✉ Via dei Magazzini Generali 8 € €5-10 ☽ 10pm-4am Tue-Sun Sep-May ☒ to Via Ostiense

Fonclea (4, C2)

The best place for a night out in the Borgo, this is a popular pub-venue with nightly live music, be it jazz, soul, funk or rock (often cover bands). Also serves up reasonable Italian and Mexican food.
☎ 06 689 63 02 ✉ Via Crescenzio 82a € up to €6 ☽ 7pm-2am Sep-May; shows 10pm ☒ to Piazza del Risorgimento

Forte Prenestino (3, F4)

One of the most bizarrely set social centres, in a huge 19th-century fortress complete with a moat and winding passages. Forte Prenestino houses all sorts of counterculture events, from gigs to punk circus acts.
☎ 06 218 07 855 ☐ www .forteprenestino.net ✉ Via Federico Delpino 100 € around €5 ☽ varies ☒ 🚃 to Via Prenestina

Goa (3, C7)

Best and hippest of Rome's big clubs, with big-gun DJs, Goa is slinky industrial-oriental, decked in reds, purples and plasma screens, with comfy couches to sink into. Expect housey tunes and power-happy bouncers.
☎ 06 574 82 77 ✉ Via Giuseppe Libetta 13 € €15 ☽ 11pm-4am Wed-Sun Oct-Apr Ⓜ Garbatella

La Maison (6, A2)
Banquettes, chandeliers and terrific sounds make this the perfect *centro storico* late-night spot when you're not in the mood for doof-doof. Good-looking, flirty 30-somethings dominate. Take at least four hours to get ready and expect anything from funk to bossa nova. Some summers it moves to the terrace of Mussolini's Palace of Justice in EUR.
☎ 06 683 33 12 ⊠ Vicolo dei Granari 4 € free but drinks are expensive 🕙 11.30pm-4am Tue-Sun Sep-May, Fri & Sat Jun-Aug 🚍 to Corso Vittorio Emanuele II

Locanda Atlantide (3, D4)
A battered door hides this popular, grungy San Lorenzo haunt, with old bikes and prams decorating the well-priced bar. It gets packed with punters appreciating the frequent live acts from punk to ska, DJs to theatre.
☎ 06 447 045 40 ⊠ Via dei Lucani 22B € up to €5 🕙 10pm-4am Tue-Sun Oct–mid-June Ⓜ Vittorio Emanuelle

Metaverso (2, A5)
This is easily Monte Testaccio's coolest choice, a tiny arched cellar club that gets very busy. Music policy trips from reggae to dub to '70s disco funk and hip hop, with a friendly crowd appreciating the cheap drinks.
☎ 06 574 47 12 🖳 www .metaverso.com ⊠ Via di Monte Testaccio € €5 🕙 10pm-6am 🚍 🚋 to Via Marmorata

Micca Club (3, E4)
Dazzlingly designed Micca Club fills a series of pop-art, brick-arched cellars. It's dedicated to the '60s and '70s, but isn't a nostalgia trip (though Austin Powers types abound). Expect live jazz followed by rare '60s grooves. Book online.
☎ 06 874 40 079 🖳 www .miccaclub.com ⊠ Via Pietro Micca 7A 🕙 Thu-Sat, live act 10pm Ⓜ Termini

No Stress Brasil (3, B6)
The name says it all: forget your troubles and perfect your samba moves at this colourful, bubbly restaurant-disco with nightly live music. The Brazilian band works everyone into a frenzy before poppy DJs do their stuff.
☎ 338 234 74 60 ⊠ Via degli Stradivari 35 € dinner & show €25 🕙 8.30pm-4am 🚍 🚋 to Viale di Trastevere

Rialtosantambrogio (2, B1)
A ghetto-tastic social centre, this feels like you have stumbled into an art college, but is an alternative, city-centre melting pot, with popular club nights, art exhibitions, live music and cinema.
☎ 06 68 13 36 40 🖳 www .rialtosantambrogio.org ⊠ Via Sant'Ambrogio 4 € around €5 🕙 various 🚋 to Largo Argentina

Testaccio Village (2, A6)
What you can do with an open street! Every summer this Testaccio corner fills with food stalls, bars, clubs (from poppy to reggae) and live music. It's like a music festival crossed with a club convention.
☎ 06 573 014 20 ⊠ Viale del Campo Boario € various 🕙 7pm-2am Jun-Sep 🚍 23, 75, 280, 716 Ⓜ Piramide

Villaggio Globale (2, A5)
A grungy dive, this is one of Rome's oldest social centres, in Testaccio's sometime slaughterhouse, long mooted for redevelopment. Tarantela, techno, ragga, contemporary art and much more are on offer, with occasional big names in its huge circus tent (Spazio Boario).
☎ 06 575 72 33 🖳 www .ecn.org/villaggioglobale, Italian only ⊠ Lungotevere Testaccio € from €2 🕙 varies Sep-Jul 🚍 to Lungotevere Testaccio Ⓜ Piramide

---

AT THE SOCIAL
Rome's alternative side is its unique *centro sociale* (social centre) scene. In the 1970s squatters took over various disused public buildings and turned them into entertainment venues, regularly battling with the police. Now some are long-established enough to be part of the establishment, but still offer Rome's most unusual, offbeat and cutting-edge entertainment – including gigs, club nights, cinema and exhibitions. They're also cheap, in accordance with their ethic of accessible culture. Check listings for what's on, or www.tmcrew.org for venues. Best-known are Rialtosantambrogio (below), Brancaleone (p91), Villaggio Globale (right) and Forte Prenestino (opposite).

GAY & LESBIAN ROME

Rome's gay scene is out of the closet but remains well away from the limelight. However, there's a strong core of old faithfuls and new venues opening and various one-off gay nights. Check local listings for current moves and grooves, and see p115 for more information. Capitoline Hill's Monte Caprino side is known for after-dark delights.

Rome also boasts a gay beach, Il Buco (the hole), 9km south of Lido di Ostia.

L'Alibi (2, A5)
Long Rome's premier gay venue L'Alibi nowadays attracts a mixed crowd, especially in summer (when the roof terrace opens up). There's plenty of good music – including old house, disco and frequent live acts – across two levels.
☎ 06 574 34 48 ✉ Via di Monte Testaccio 44 € Fri & Sat €10-15 ⏲ 11.30pm-5am Wed-Sun Ⓜ Piramide

Use dancing all night as your alibi at L'Alibi

FEELING HOT, HOT, HOT

Gay saunas open from 2pm or 3pm until very late and admission costs around €15 with an Arci-Gay card (available at the saunas). You could try
Europa Multiclub (☎ 06 482 36 50; Via Aureliana 40)
Apollion (☎ 06 482 53 89; Via Mecenate 59a)
Rio's Sauna (☎ 06 781 47 828; www.riossauna.it; Via dei Colli Albani 10)
Sauna Mediterraneo (☎ 06 772 05 934; Via Villari 3)

Alpheus (2, B6)
Opposite the old gasworks in Ostiense, this huge three-room dance club, with plenty of kitsch and cabaret, gets busy on gay Fridays, with the Mucca Assassina (Cow Murderer) DJ crew (moving to the Ostia beaches in summer).
☎ 06 574 78 26 ✉ Via del Commercio 36 € €8-15 ⏲ 10pm-4.30am Fri Ⓜ Piramide

Coming Out (5, A6)
Relaxed, colourful and vibrant, this cheery pub near the Colosseum is a popular meeting place for young gays and lesbians with live entertainment on Thursdays.
☎ 06 700 98 71 ✉ Via di San Giovanni in Laterano 8 € free ⏲ 5pm-5am 🚌 🚊 Via Labicana

Garbo & You (2, A2)
Camp and cosy – all red velvet, red fairylights and gilt mirrors – this snug bar is more about couples than cruising. It receives a steady flow of local and foreign gay men although it's not exclusive.
☎ 06 581 27 66 ✉ Vicolo di Santa Margherita 1a € free ⏲ 10pm-2am Tue-Sun 🚌 🚊 to Viale di Trastevere

Gay Village (3, D6)
Come summer, Gay Village takes over a 6.5 hectare site of historic parkland and transforms it into a pink outdoor entertainment complex with bars, clubs, a gym, cinema and exhibition space.
☎ 340 542 30 08 💻 www.gayvillage.it ✉ Parco San Sebastiano, entrance Via delle Terme di Caracalla 55 € varies ⏲ 7pm-2am Jun-Sep 🚌 to Terme di Caracalla

Hangar (5, A5)
Rome's oldest gay bar, American-run, is still one of its most popular – women and men are welcome, though Monday is men only. With a darkroom, it mostly gathers a mixed Italian and international crowd and gets packed at weekends.
☎ 06 488 13 97 ✉ Via in Selci 69 € free ⏲ 10.30pm-2.30am Wed-Mon Ⓜ Cavour

Max's Bar (3, D4)
A gay Rome institution, informal Max's is mainstream and popular with the full spectrum of gay men – particularly the more mature. It has great disco tunes and no attitude.
☎ 06 702 01 599 ✉ Via Achille Grandi 3a € €5-10 ⏲ 8pm-2am Tue-Sun 🚌 Ⓜ Manzoni

SPORT

Football

Il calcio (soccer) inspires more passion than politics, religion, dressing up and mama's cooking rolled into one. If you're a sports fan keen to sample the pizzazz of Serie A football, you're going to love Rome. With two top-flight teams (Roma and Lazio), the city hosts at least one match every weekend from September to June. Roma's star player is international striker Francesco Totti, a local boy from Testaccio. Lazio are one of the powerhouses of Italian football, despite its former president Sergio Cragnotti having been arrested for corruption. Both clubs have about 50,000 season ticket holders, though it's easier to get tickets for Lazio games. Attending a match is thrilling, though some rougher elements can supply an edgy atmosphere. Buy tickets direct from **Stadio Olimpico** (3, A1; ☎ 06 3 68 51; Viale dello Stadio Olimpico).

Tennis

Many of the world's best players come to Rome in May to take part in the Italian Open at **Foro Italico** (3, A1; ☎ 06 368 58 218; Viale del Foro Italico). Book weeks ahead for the final days else tickets can usually be bought on the day.

ROMAN RIVALRIES

Roma and Lazio football loyalties are split down political lines. Lazio's fans traditionally come from nearby provincial towns, and have an unfortunate (but deserved) reputation for racism and fascist sympathies — player Paolo Di Canio extended his right arm in what he described as a 'Roman salute' after scoring in the 2005 derby. Roma's supporters, known as *romanisti*, are historically working class, from Rome's Jewish community, Trastevere and Testaccio.

If you're still undecided about which team to support, Lazio wear stylish light blue while the Roma colours are deep red with natty orange trim. Lazio has the better chants, while Roma has the most passionate supporters and the loudest fireworks.

So, if you go to the Stadio Olimpico, bear in mind that Roma fans flock to the Curva Sud (southern stand) while Lazio supporters stand in the Curva Nord (northern stand).

You'll need to pick your team – AS Roma fans (pictured) are truly devoted

Rugby Union

For three weekends during February and March, Rome is swamped by thousands of fans, many with a penchant for silly hats. Since 2000 Italy has been entered into the Six Nations Rugby Championships (against England, France, Ireland, Scotland and Wales) with games at **Stadio Flaminio** (3, B2; ☎ 06 323 65 39; Viale Tiziano).

Equestrian

The **Piazza di Siena** (3, C3; ☎ 06 322 53 57; www.piazzadisiena.com) show jumping competition has been held in Villa Borghese for over 70 years.

Sleeping

From gilt-laden *palazzi* and conceptual-designer comfort to quaint hotels, pint-sized *pensioni* and cheery hostels, Rome has good lodgings in every price bracket. For these, you have to book well in advance – the Eternal City is a popular destination year-round (though particularly from April to June, September, October and Christmas when prices are often 30% higher). At the most expensive hotels you can sometimes get reductions from the rack rate – ask about promotions.

You'll get more comfort for your buck outside the *centro storico* (historic city centre), but staying in an atmospheric area a stone's throw from the sights, can be well worth the extra outlay. Around Campo de' Fiori is pretty but can be noisy at night, while Trastevere is a charming option, but has fewer hotels. There are some lovely hotels in peaceful Aventino, and the genteel Borgo (near the Vatican) is another quiet option. Around Stazione Termini you'll find the cheapest hotels, but it's also less picturesque and can feel dodgy at night (lone women might feel more comfortable elsewhere).

The one- to five-star rating relates to facilities only and gives no indication of value, comfort, atmosphere or friendliness. Standards here can trail behind international expectations. Rooms in converted *palazzi* are often small (albeit luxurious), and there are seldom gyms and pools. Deluxe and many top-end hotels provide minibar, air-con, fine linen, 24-hour room service and private baths with hairdryers and bathrobes. Facilities are more basic in midrange places; you won't always find a hairdryer, minibar, room service or even air-conditioning. The only guarantee at budget places is a bed and a roof. The air-con question is an important one from June to August, when the city sizzles.

Breakfast in cheaper accommodation is rarely worth a bleary eye so, if you have the option, save a few bob and pop into a bar for a coffee and *cornetto* (croissant) as the Romans do.

ROOM RATES

These categories indicate the cost per night of a standard double room in high season.

Deluxe	from €280
Top End	€190-280
Midrange	€100-190
Budget	under €100

Hallway at Hotel Celio (p98)

DELUXE

Art by the Spanish Steps
(4, F1)

Startling contemporary style here is melded onto a historic building. Plexiglass bubbles fill the vaulted lobby and the bar is housed in a chapel. The smallish rooms are sharply designed, but simpler, with parquet and modern wooden furniture. Soundproofing is not great.

☎ 06 32 87 11 🖳 www
.hotelart.it ✉ Via Margutta
56 Ⓜ Spagna ♿ good
✕ p74

Hassler Villa Medici
(4, G2)

JFK, Elizabeth Taylor and various royal families have bedded down at the glitteringly glamorous Hassler, at the top of the Spanish Steps. The atmosphere is all chandelier-glinting splendour, and rooms strikingly decorated, especially those in black, white and red. The rooftop restaurant has stupendous views, and there's a courtyard bar.

☎ 06 69 93 40 🖳 www
.hotelhasslerroma.com
✉ Piazza della Trinitá

dei Monti 6 Ⓜ Spagna
♿ ✕ rooftop restaurant

Hotel de Russie (4, F1)

Once a palace, this is now A-list heaven, where visiting celebrities swan when they're in town, with Leonardo di Caprio, George Clooney, Brad Pitt among recent guests. It's sumptuous, subtly decorated, and impeccable, backed by marvellous terraced gardens up to the Pincio.

☎ 06 32 88 81 🖳 www.roc
cofortehotels.com ✉ Via del
Babuino 9 🖳 to Via del Corso
Ⓜ Flaminio ♿ ✕ restaur-
ant & Stravinsky Bar

Hotel d'Inghilterra
(4, F2)

Well-located in Tridente, wood-panelled, gilt-edged and exclusive, this is a stately and elegant blast from the past. Liszt, Mendelssohn and Hemingway have all hunkered down at d'Inghilterra.

☎ 06 699 81 204 🖳 www
.hir.royaldemeure.com
✉ Via Bocca di Leone 14
Ⓜ Spagna ♿ ✕ p74

Hotel Eden (4, G2)

Swish, classic and luxurious, but unstuffy, the Eden is

situated on a hilltop close to Villa Borghese so most rooms have splendid views over Rome (the ones at the front over the city itself). There's a marvellous rooftop restaurant and bar.

☎ 06 47 81 21 🖳 www
.hotel-eden.it ✉ Via
Ludovisi 49 Ⓜ Barberini
♿ ✕ La Terrazza restaur-
ant & Il Salotto

Inn at the Spanish Steps
(4, G2)

A discreet doorway next to Café Greco leads to this discovery, a luxurious boutique guesthouse, in the 17th-century house where Hans Christian Andersen once lived, with small but impressive antique-filled rooms. There's a lovely tree-shaded terrace for breakfast and *aperitivo*. Suites and apartments overlooking the Spanish Steps are also available.

☎ 06 699 25 657 🖳 www
.atspanishsteps.com ✉ Via
Condotti 85 Ⓜ Spagna
✕ p74

Radisson SAS (5, C4)

Previously Hotel Es, this is a five-star futuristic, minimalist dream, with luminous reception desks like spaceship consoles and cool sci-fi (though smallish) rooms to make you feel like you're living in *Wallpaper** magazine. After dark the inner atrium glows polychromatic patchwork, and the rooftop bar (see p90) is a sexy place for an *aperitivo*.

☎ 06 44 48 41 🖳 www
.rome.radissonsas.com
✉ Via Filippo Turati 171
🚇 to Via Napoleone III
Ⓜ Termini ♿ ✕ Sette

Have a *Star Trek* experience at Radisson SAS

TOP END

Aventino Sant'Anselmo
(2, B4)

If you want olde-worlde charm, affordable luxury and quieter surroundings, these four separate Art Nouveau villas — each with gardens and courtyards — are situated on the leafy and affluent Aventine hill, near lovely Santa Sabina. The villas have great views over Rome, and are a short walk to Testaccio. ☎ 06 57 00 57 🖥 www .aventinohotels.com ✉ Piazza di Sant'Anselmo 2 🚍 to Via Marmorata Ⓜ Circo Massimo ✗ p83

Casa Howard (4, G3)

A gorgeous boutique guesthouse, this has two branches near the Spanish Steps, each with five richly decorated rooms. At Capo le Case, only two are ensuite (others have detached bathrooms, and kimonos and slippers are provided for the short walk). Hotel de Russie—designer Tommaso Ziffer decked out the Sistina branch, where all rooms are ensuite. ☎ 06 699 24 555 🖥 www .casahoward.com ✉ Via Capo le Case 18, Via Sistina Ⓜ Spagna 🚻 👍 ✗ p74

APARTMENT RENTAL

Renting an apartment can be an excellent idea and may work out cheaper than a city-centre hotel, particularly for families. Expect to pay a minimum of €775 a month (plus bills and a hefty deposit) for a studio apartment or a small one-bedroom place near the centre of town. Try the fortnightly listing magazine *Wanted in Rome* (from newsstands; www.wantedinrome.com) or www .romanreference.com and www.romecityapartments .com. The Beehive runs a reservation system to find homestays, B&Bs and apartments, check it out at www .cross-pollinate.com. Hotel Campo de' Fiori also offers some snug apartments around il Campo, check www .hotelcampodefiori.it.

Hotel Bramante (4, B3)

Near the Vatican, this charming restored 16th-century building was home to the Swiss architect, Domenico Fontana, and has beamed wooden ceilings. It was converted into a hostel for pilgrims in the 19th century, and is comfortable and elegant, with marble bathrooms and antique furnishings. ☎ 06 688 06 426 🖥 www .travel.it/roma/bramante/ ✉ Vicolo delle Palline 24 🚍 to Piazza del Risorgimento 👍 ✗ p80

Hotel Celio (4, J6)

Celio is a mad mix of rococo, frescos, mosaics, velvets,

Aptly named Hotel Forum

eclectic antiques and red flock: a small, artsy hotel next to the Colosseum. Each of the gorgeous rooms are named after famous artists. Bathrooms are notably bijou. ☎ 06 704 95 333 🖥 www .hotelcelio.com ✉ Via dei Santissimi Quattro 35c 🚍 Ⓜ Colosseo 👍 ✗ p77

Hotel Forum (4, H5)

A smart, staid, small hotel, with antique-dotted lounges and big, cosy rooms in a former convent. The selling point is the delightful rooftop restaurant and terrace bar

One of the lavishly decorated rooms at Casa Howard

(open May to October), with breathtaking views over ancient Rome.

☎ 06 679 24 46 🖳 www .hotelforumrome.com ✉ Via Tor de' Conti 25-30 🚌 to Via dei Fori Imperiali Ⓜ Cavour ⊠ rooftop

Hotel Santa Maria Trastevere (2, A2)

With legions of satisfied customers, this is a leafy haven in central Trastevere. You enter via an ivy-lined drive, to find rooms arranged hacienda-style around an orange tree–filled courtyard (where breakfast is served when the weather is good). Rooms are decorated in comfortable, peachy, country-house chic and are good for families, some sleeping up to six.

☎ 06 589 46 26 🖳 www .htlsantamaria.com ✉ Vicolo del Piede 2 🚆 Viale Trastevere ♿ excellent 👶 ⊠ p77

MIDRANGE

Albergo del Sole (6, B4)

Dating to 1462, this is Rome's oldest hotel, with a great location off Campo de' Fiori. All that history is not reflected in the rooms, which are perfectly pleasant, but functional. The view over the cobbled street is romantic but can be noisy late at night, in this, one of Rome's most happening districts after dark.

☎ 06 687 94 46 🖳 info@ solealbiscione.it ✉ Via del Biscione 76 🚌 to Corso Vittorio Emanuelle II ⊠ p69

Daphne Veneto (4, H2)

American Italian–run Daphne is a luxurious

Sleep like Caesar at Hotel Celio

boutique B&B, with delightful contemporary, very comfortable rooms, all browns, creams and bronzes. Multilingual staff are very helpful and you get a mobile phone to borrow during your visit. There's another branch (Daphne Trevi) at Via degli Avignonesi 20 (4, H3; same phone number).

☎ 06 478 23 529 🖳 www .daphne-rome.com ✉ Via di San Basilio 55 Ⓜ Barberini ⊠ p81

Hotel d'Este (5, B4)

This calm, charming hotel is convenient for its proximity to Santa Maria Maggiore and nearby churches. Rooms are a bit dowdy but pleasantly old-fashioned and some have

small balconies overlooking the busy street and up to the huge basilica. Friendly staff work hard to please.

☎ 06 446 56 07 🖳 www .hotel-deste.com ✉ Via Carlo Alberto 6 Ⓜ Vittorio Emanuele ⊠ p81

Hotel Locarno (4, E1)

An Art-Deco gem ideally placed for Tridente, this has bags of character and a marvellous entrance, bar and small garden. Rooms are a bit disappointing and fusty (best are those in the new wing), but the rest is great and the welcome friendly.

☎ 06 361 08 41 🖳 www .hotellocarno.com ✉ Via della Penna 22 🚌 to Via di Ripetta Ⓜ Flaminio ⊠ p74

Enjoy a friendly reception at Hotel d'Este (p99)

Hotel Margutta (4, F1)
In the thick of the fashion district, a stiletto-hop from Via Condotti, Margutta is a small, old-fashioned hotel, with basic, slightly old-fashioned and pokey but fresh rooms. The friendly management deserve another star.
☎ 06 322 36 74; fax 06 320 0395 ✉ Via Laurina 34 Ⓜ Spagna ✖ p74

Hotel Modigliani (4, H2)
Lots of contented customers rate this charming place, run by an Italian artist-writer couple, with grey, spacious, light rooms; there's a quiet internal courtyard for drinks. Top-floor superior rooms have smashing views.
☎ 06 428 15 226 ⌨ www .hotelmodigliani.com ✉ Via della Purificazione 42 Ⓜ Barberini ♿ ✖ p81

Hotel Teatro di Pompeo (6, B4)
In one of Rome's most colourful neighbourhoods, this old charmer is built on the ruins of the 1st-century-BC

Theatre of Pompey – where Caesar was murdered. Rooms are comfortable and old-fashioned, as if they haven't had a refit since the 1950s.
☎ 06 687 28 12; fax 06 688 05 531 ✉ Largo del Pallaro 8 🚌 to Corso Vittorio Emanuelle II ♿ ✖ p69

Hotel Trastevere (4, D6)
Somewhat out of the way in Trastevere, yet close to its picturesque heart, this plain place has nine functional, bright, clean rooms, some with views over the neighbouring (but not overwhelmingly pretty) piazza. Independent apartments are also available. Prices are bottom of the bracket.
☎ 06 581 47 13 ⌨ info@ hoteltrastevere.net ✉ Via Luciano Manara 24a-25 🚌 🚋 Piazza Sonnino ✖ p77

Nicolas Inn (4, H5)
A friendly welcome from a charming, helpful couple awaits at this nice, popular 1st-floor guesthouse. Rooms are sparklingly clean and spa-

cious and well-soundproofed.
☎ 06 976 18 483 ⌨ www .nicolasinn.com ✉ Via Cavour 295 🚌 to Metro Colosseo ✖ p77

BUDGET

Arena House (4, J6)
A hidden, backstreet, family-run guesthouse, this has basic rooms overlooking neighbouring gardens, and helpful, friendly owners and a good location near the Colosseum.
☎ 06 976 15 384 ⌨ www .arena-house.com ✉ Via Marco Aurelio 37 Ⓜ Colosseo ✖ p77

Beehive (5, B3)
If a boutique hostel sounds like a contradiction in terms, stay at the American-run Beehive and have a rethink. This is a stunning place with bright fresh dorms, jazzily bright-white contemporary doubles (with shared bath), a stylish garden terrace, great café, free Internet and local phone calls and lots of local information.
☎ 06 447 04553 ⌨ www .the-beehive.com ✉ Via

Marghera 8 Ⓜ Termini
♿ ✕ Café

Carmel (3, B5)
Good-value Carmel is a kosher hotel on a pretty, tree-lined street, close to the charms of Trastevere. Rooms are basic but clean, and there's a beautifully shady roof terrace.
☎ 06 580 99 21; fax 06 581 88 53 ✉ Via Goffredo Mameli 11 🚌 🚊 Viale di Trastevere ✕ p77

Casa Kolbe (2, C2)
A former Franciscan monastery, opposite the Palatine, here you can live in monkish comfort (if the weather's not too hot) in the spartan rooms. There's a large sheltered garden and it's a great location: a quiet but central area of the city. Try to get a room overlooking the garden. It is named after a former resident, a Polish monk who was killed in Auschwitz. Groups often take it over.
☎ 06 679 49 74; fax 06 599 41 550 ✉ Via di San Teodoro 44 🚌 to Via dei Cerchi ✕ p77

Fawlty Towers (5, B3)
Longstanding and popular, this 5th-floor (with a lift) hostel offers small dorms, clean bathrooms and a kitchen and common room with lots of facilities. There's small sunny terrace too. Book well in advance for private rooms and the night before for dorms. Check out at 9am.
☎ /fax 06 445 03 74 🖳 www.fawltytowers .org ✉ Via Magenta 39 Ⓜ Termini ✕ p81

BED & BREAKFAST
Relatively new to Rome, B&Bs offer a more personable approach to accommodation. Frequently you'll be staying in a family house, usually spotlessly clean and offering a cosy alternative to a hotel. However, bear in mind, keys are often not provided, and they are probably not a good idea for night owls. **Bed & Breakfast Italy** (www.bed-and-breakfast-in-Italy.com) or **Bed & Breakfast in Italy** (www.bbitalia.com) are booking agencies, or try the Chamber of Commerce (who vets the accommodation; www.bedroma.com). You could also try www.cross-pollinate.com.

Hotel Colors (4, C2)
Clean, bright and friendly, this hostel is in a quiet area near the Vatican and offers small dorms and some private rooms (with air-con) all brightly painted as per the name, and a terrace. Note that it's on the 6th floor without a lift.
☎ 06 687 40 30 🖳 www .colorshotel.com ✉ Via Boezio 31 Ⓜ Ottaviano ✕ self-catering kitchen & p80

Hotel Lady (4, C1)
This one-floor peaceful pension is run by a warmly welcoming Roman couple who don't speak much English but don't let language barriers get in the way of friendly chat. Two of the pleasant rooms have original beamed ceilings, and the (mostly) shared bathrooms are modern and clean.
☎ 06 324 21 12; fax 06 324 34 46 ✉ Via Germanico 198 🚌 70, 186, 280, 913 Ⓜ Lepanto ✕ p80

Hotel Panda (4, F2)
This is one of the best pensions in Rome; it's cheap, close to the Spanish Steps, has pretty rooms (ensuite and with shared bathroom), some with frescoed and some with beamed ceilings (but some very small), with good bathrooms with the occasional alcove sculpture, and hospitable English-speaking staff. Book ahead because the secret's out.
☎ 06 678 01 79 🖳 www .hotelpanda.it ✉ Via della Croce 35 🚌 to Via del Corso Ⓜ Spagna ✕ p74

Hotel Panda is a rare find

About Rome

HISTORY
The Foundation of Rome

According to legend, abandoned twins Romulus and Remus (offspring of Mars), had a stroke of luck when they were adopted by a kindly she-wolf. The brothers later fought over the governing rights of a new settlement – no prizes for guessing who survived – and Rome was founded on 21 April 753 BC, still celebrated as the city's birthday.

The historic facts of Rome's foundation are more tricky to pin down, although we know that 9th-century-BC huts were discovered on the Palatine and the first documented rulers were Etruscans. Their kingdom lasted until 507 BC, when Tarquin the Proud fell out with the Romans, who revolted and established the Republic.

The Rise of the Roman Empire

Rome prospered, controlled by the most powerful clans. Two elected consuls guided the Senate – a council of elders from the most important families – following a policy of divide and conquer. The Etruscans were assimilated, surrounding tribes allied and Rome's influence extended rapidly. With its eventual victory in the Punic wars over Carthage, Rome dominated the Mediterranean. It became a city based on militarism, mainly inhabited by soldiers and merchants living off the proceeds of war and empire.

A discontented general, Gaius Julius Caesar, defied the city fathers by bringing his army into Italy – by 'crossing the Rubicon' border – and wrested power. He led Rome for six years before his assassination in 44 BC. After almost two decades of civil war his nephew, Octavian (using the title Augustus), defeated Mark Antony and his pharaoh half, Cleopatra, to become Rome's first emperor. He encouraged the equation of emperor and god.

Rome prospered, largely from the exploitation of its vast empire which peaked over the next century, during the reigns of Trajan and Hadrian of the Flavian dynasty. By this time Rome had 1.5 million residents (an urban population unrivalled anywhere until the 19th century), placated with a diet of 'bread and circuses', free grain and the kind of entertainment that took place in the Colosseum. But with Emperor Marcus Aurelius' death in AD 180, Rome's fortunes began to reverse and repeated Barbarian invasions began to take their toll.

Anyone for cricket? Tempio di Vespasiano at the Roman Forum

The threat was such that Emperor Aurelian fortified the city in the 3rd century with the Aurelian Wall, which still stands today.

The Fall of the Roman Empire

As sprawling territories became more difficult to defend, it made less sense to have Rome as the capital and the Empire was divided by Diocletian. His successor, Constantine, converted to Christianity in 312 and gave the religion its first foothold, donating land to the Bishop of Rome to build a basilica – San Giovanni in Laterano. However, when he moved his power base to Byzantium (now Istanbul) in 330, Rome's period as *caput mundi* (capital of the world) came to an end. The Goths and Vandals sacked the city in the 5th century.

MAD EMPERORS

Megalomaniac Roman leaders indulged in often psychotic excesses. One of the worst was Caligula ('Little Shoes'; AD 37–41), who specialised in extravagance, extortion and murder. He was in love with his sister and legend has it wanted to make his horse a senator (which may have been to show his derision for the Senate). Nero (AD 54–68), Augustus' last descendant, started well but then became famously nasty. As well as murdering relatives and rivals, the tyrant taxed his subjects to build his huge palace, Domus Aurea, possibly started the fire that destroyed two-thirds of Rome in AD 64 *and* insisted on declaiming his own terrible poetry.

Christian Rome & the Middle Ages

By the 6th century Rome was a desolate shadow, chaotic and dangerous, with a population of around 80,000 living among its ruins. Gregory I's papacy (590–604) rescued Rome from demise. By negotiating with invaders, building basilicas and attracting pilgrims, he brought political clout back to the city. Its place as centre of the Christian world was cemented when Pope Leo III allied with the Franks and crowned Charlemagne Holy Roman Emperor in 800. The papacy was by now a big prize for Europe's powerbrokers and the French temporarily took control of it when the papal court was relocated to Avignon from 1309–1379.

Timeless ecclesiastical fashion

Counter-Reformation, the Papacy & the Arts

In the 15th century the papacy moved to the safer situation of the Vatican. Popes gradually rebuilt Rome, spending some of the vast wealth amassed from taxing the Catholic world. While most Romans lived in poverty, the popes enjoyed incredible luxury and summoned leading Renaissance artists to redecorate.

Pope Clement VII unwisely sided against the Holy Roman Emperor Charles V of Spain, whose forces plundered the city in 1527. Remarkably, the Papacy survived repeated power struggles, internal corruption and the Reformation sparked by Martin Luther's protests against church excesses.

After the sack of Rome by Charles V's forces, the city had to be rebuilt and the Counter Reformation began in response to Protestantism. New groups like the Jesuits were encouraged, and splendid, awe-inspiring churches built (like Il Gesù, p33) to attract people back to Catholicism. Renaissance tolerance gave way to persecution of intellectuals, such as Galileo Galilei (1564–1642). The Inquisition (the suppression of supposed heretics) went into overdrive and executions were commonplace. Pope Paul IV confined Jews to the Ghetto in 1556.

In the 17th century the popes recruited baroque masters such as Bernini and Borromini, overspending wildly, and sending the economy into decline. However, the following century this investment started paying dividends and the first waves of friendly invaders, the Grand Tourists, arrived. These were wealthy Europeans who indulged in an international 'grand tour' to complete their education.

Fresco commemorating the Catholic victory over the Protestants in 1620 in Santa Maria della Vittoria

Napoleonic Occupation

Over the centuries the popes had acquired provinces in central Italy known as the Papal States, with Rome as capital. The prize attracted Napoleon, who occupied the city in 1798, bringing the Vatican to its knees. He crowned himself king of Italy in 1805, demanded the pope's abdication and annexed Rome three years later.

Unification

After Napoleon's defeat, Italy was restored to its conglomeration of small princely states. However, change was afoot, and patriots Giuseppe Mazzini and Giuseppe Garibaldi led the unification movement. In 1861 the Kingdom of Italy was declared under King Vittorio Emanuele II, although the by-then French-supported pope was still sovereign of Rome. Troops stormed the city in 1870 and Rome became capital, ushering in a 30-year building boom.

Fascism & WWII

Social unrest after WWI paved the way for Benito Mussolini and his Fascist Party. Inspired by ancient Rome, he bulldozed huge sweeping roads between Rome's greatest monuments, and created a new obelisk-decorated suburb, EUR (p38), complete with a new Colosseum. In 1929, Il Duce (the leader) and Pope Pius XI signed the Lateran Pact, declaring Catholicism Italy's sole religion and recognising the Vatican as an independent state.

When push came to shove in WWII, fascist Italy withered. Mussolini was executed by firing squad in Milan in 1945 and his body was hung upside down in Piazzale Loreto and pelted with stones. In 1946, Italy abolished the monarchy by referendum and the royal family was sent into exile (only allowed to return, as private citizens, in 2003).

Modern Times

Rome hosted the Olympic Games in 1960, but the following two decades were blighted by student and worker revolts, and occasional terrorism. The growth of the 1980s was undone in the 1990s when unemployment soared, the lira floundered and government corruption was exposed. It began the millennium with a bang: a massive refurbishment of tourist attractions and infrastructure. In recent years, leftwing Mayor Walter Veltroni has overseen an explosion in the arts scene that has made the city more vibrant than at any time since la dolce vita.

IL CAVALIERE

Pancake-faced and gaffe-prone Berlusconi may be, but he has amassed a US$10 billion fortune, owns most of the Italian media and has headed the longest-serving Italian government since WWII. Coming from an ordinary middle-class background, he undoubtedly turns all he touches to gold. Unfortunately this has tended to benefit him rather than the Italian populace. Perhaps it's Italian cynicism that has allowed such a figure retain power (piove, governo ladro, the proverb goes – it rains, the government steals). Or perhaps it is admiration: in the land where furbo (cunning) is admired, he is the most furbo of all.

ENVIRONMENT

Traffic and air pollution are Rome's greatest environmental hazards. Efforts to reduce traffic have increased dramatically of late: special permits are needed to drive in the city centre, on certain days only odd or even numberplates are permitted to ease congestion, strict regulations govern levels of

gas emissions from motor vehicles and *motorini* (scooters), public transport is slowly being upgraded and there's a small network of electric buses. Despite these measures, many city monuments – and the health and enjoyment of visitors – are still at risk from pollution.

GOVERNMENT & POLITICS

Rome's municipal government is headed by a *sindaco* (mayor) elected by the public, currently Walter Veltroni of the Democratici di Sinistra (DS democracy of the left) party while Lazio regional council president is Francesco Storace from the far-right Alleanza Nazionale party.

Rome is also the seat of national government and capital of the *regione* of Lazio. A parliamentary republic, Italy is headed by a president, who appoints the prime minister. The parliament consists of two houses – a Senate and a Chamber of Deputies – both with equal legislative power.

From 2001, a parliamentary conservative coalition was headed

Guarding the Palazzo del Quirinale (p38)

by Silvio Berlusconi, a controversial figure who also heads a vast media business empire (as if Rupert Murdoch were elected British Prime Minister). In 2006 he narrowly lost the election to Romano Prodi, who steers a left-wing coalition government.

ECONOMY

Tourism generates over 10% of Rome's economy and is on the rise, with the rest coming from banking, fashion, insurance, printing and publishing. Employment in the capital is largely based on Italy's bloated state bureaucracy. Many Romans working in the private sector are self employed. Bucking the trend in the rest of Italy, the economy is looking robust, with unemployment lower than for several years.

SOCIETY & CULTURE

Rome's ageing population mirrors Italy's demographic trend, the only country in the world where the old outnumber the young. The population is increasing, however, thanks to the influx of immigrants. Official records suggest around 200,000 of the population are foreigners, although the number is probably considerably higher if you take illegal immigrants into account. Locals and immigrants coexist peacefully, although communities don't tend to integrate and incidences of intolerance and xenophobia are not uncommon.

Some 84% of Italians are Catholic (but only 34% attend church regularly) with the remainder made up of Muslims (around 1.3 million), Protestants and Jews.

A frequent sight in Christendom's capital

Despite falling birth rates – which demographers warn could lead to the extinction of the Italian in 200 years if not reversed! – the family is the bedrock of Roman and Italian society. The majority stay in the family home until their 30s, a situation exacerbated by unemployment and house prices. Even then, one in three still see mamma every day.

High prices in the city are leading people, particularly the young, to move out of town. Between 1991 and 2001 Rome's population fell by 6.8% and still it continues to fall, albeit slowly.

Etiquette

Centuries of visiting *stranieri* (foreigners) have accustomed Romans to their weird ways, and it's difficult to faux pas. People don't expect you to speak Italian although they will warm to you much quicker – and even charge you less – if you try a few phrases.

The most common way tourists offend local sensibilities – apart from their fashion sense – is by baring flesh. You won't be allowed into some churches if you're inadequately attired. Cover your shoulders, knees and don a little respect and sensitivity.

When greeting people (friends of friends) you've already met, a glancing kiss on each cheek is customary. With strangers, it's fine to shake hands.

Romans don't generally drink much alcohol and getting drunk – especially if you're a woman – is frowned upon.

Smoking is prohibited in public offices, on public transport, and in all bars, cafés and restaurants. Despite their often take-it-or-leave-it attitude to official rulings, Romans do abide by this one.

ARTS

Rome showcases almost three millennia of the most beautiful things ever made, and all made here: from Etruscan pottery to Michelangelo's frescoes, from Roman temples to Bernini's sculptures. Like Rome itself, its art is often formed of layers of history, with Roman doors and columns used to construct churches, ancient statues improved with baroque additions, and imperial baths used to make fountains.

Etruscan

The sophisticated Etruscans surpassed the Romans artistically – this wealthy civilisation produced an incredible array of vibrant, sensuous arts. Although no Etruscan buildings survive in Rome, the Museo Nazionale Etrusco di Villa Giulia (p23) contains a fantastic array of artefacts, including exquisite gold jewellery and intimate terracotta portraiture.

Etruscan-style temple roof ornament at the Museo Nazionale Etrusco di Villa Giulia

Classical Rome

Much Roman architecture was copied from the Greek or adapted from the Etruscans, but with the discovery of quick-curing concrete in the 1st century BC, the Romans perfected arches and domes, producing the triumphal arches in the Roman Forum and the remarkable domed Pantheon (p18). The Romans also built vast amphitheatres, like the Colosseum (p12), and column-lined rectangular meeting houses, known as basilicas.

The Romans inherited painting and mosaic from the Greeks and Etruscans, but improved on these arts, as can be seen in the stunning Museo Nazionale Romano's Palazzo Massimo alle Terme (p17).

Early Roman sculptures were copies of ancient Greek works, which promoted the classical ideal, like the *Gaul's Suicide* in the Palazzo Altemps (p29) and the dynamic *Laocoön* in the Vatican Museums (p10). However, busts were a Roman innovation, often realistic rather than idealised portraits, giving a fascinating view of ancient Roman physiognomy.

An unflattering portrait? Ostia Antica (p50)

Christian

From the 4th century, Christian art began to dominate. Churches followed the same shape (often occupying the same sites) as earlier basilicas. Some stunning mosaics remain, including Santa Maria Maggiore (p36), Santi Cosma e Damiano (p37) and Santa Prassede (p36). Two beautiful early churches are Santa Sabina (p36) and San Clemente (p16).

Early Christians were fond of simple mosaics, an art that was revolutionised in the 12th century

Mosaics in extraordinary San Clemente

when the Cosmati family began recycling fragments of coloured glass and marble to create intricate patterned pavements and other decoration. You'll find these in churches all over Rome.

Pietro Cavallini (1250–1330) left superb frescoes and mosaic work in the churches of Santa Cecilia (p34) and Santa Maria (p35) in Trastevere.

Renaissance

Rome was in the doldrums during the 14th century and missed out on the Gothic period, but it burst back to life in the 15th century with the Renaissance. A succession of big-spending popes lured many famous artists, and the likes of Botticelli, Ghirlandaio and Raphael all left their marks.

Classical order and proportion were the hallmarks of Renaissance architecture and Bramante (1441–1514) was its chief exponent (he spent his first four years here measuring ancient buildings). One of his finest works is his Tempietto (p39). Michelangelo (1475–1564), Renaissance master, built the 42m-wide dome over St Peter's Basilica. His work dominates the unparalleled Sistine Chapel (p10).

Counter-Reformation

The High Renaissance abruptly ended with the sacking of Rome in 1527. Rome had a brief Mannerist fling but art slumped in the 16th century. Into the void stepped Caravaggio (1573–1609) with his dramatically lit naturalism.

RENAISSANCE RIVALS

By happy accident, jealous manipulation led to the glories of the Sistine Chapel. Bramante, wishing to see his friend Raphael triumph and wonder-boy Michelangelo fail, suggested Michelangelo for the chapel because he was inexperienced in fresco. Michelangelo, the born sculptor, did his best to turn flat surfaces into three dimensions, with extraordinary results. When the work was unveiled there was a sensation. Bramante was furious, and tried to persuade the pope to take on Raphael instead. But by now the pope was convinced of Michelangelo's genius and delighted for him to continue, only wishing that he'd hurry up and pestering him to add more gold (he refused).

The stunning baroque ceiling of Santa Maria della Vittoria (p35)

Baroque

The theatrical style of 17th-century baroque had enormous impact, particularly the work produced by two bitter rivals Francesco Borromini (1599–1667) and Gian Lorenzo Bernini (1598–1680).

Borromini was a great architect who started as a stonemason, a tortured soul who broke new ground in the creation of spatial effects. Two of his most stunning works are San Carlo alle Quattro Fontane (p33) and the ingenious, illusory colonnade in Galleria Spada (p28). But Borromini lived in the shadow of dazzling all-rounder Bernini who won commissions galore though clever alliances. He transformed the city with his churches, *palazzi*, squares, and fountains, and was an extraordinarily gifted sculptor, as can be seen in his work at Galleria Borghese (p13).

Neoclassicism

The baroque love of grand gesture continued into the 18th century with the Fontana di Trevi (p40) and the Spanish Steps (p19), created for the new influx of Grand Tourists. Neoclassicism – a response to the excesses of the baroque and a nostalgic reinterpretation of ancient Greek art – was the last great movement in Rome and is best represented by the sculptor Antonio Canova (1757–1822). His most famous work is the cold, erotic portrayal of *Paolina Bonaparte Borghese* in the Galleria Borghese (p13).

Fascist & Modern

Mussolini left his architectural mark with rigid, monumental building schemes such as Stazione Termini and Esposizione Universale di Roma (EUR; p38).

More recent art movements, including the Macchiaioli post-impressionists, are exhibited in the Galleria Nazionale d'Arte Moderna (p28). With few new buildings of note in the second half of the 20th century, Rome leapt into the 21st with a flurry of new commissions: Odile Decq's MACRO (p29), Zara

Fascist architecture embodied – Palazzo della Civiltà del Lavoro (EUR)

Hadid's MAXXI (p29), both of which exhibit cutting-edge contemporary art, and Renzo Piano's Parco della Musica (p86).

ARRIVAL & DEPARTURE

You can fly direct to Rome from most European capitals, Australia, Asia, Africa and the USA, although some carriers use Milan as their Italian gateway. There are good train services linking the city to neighbouring countries.

Air
LEONARDO DA VINCI (FIUMICINO)
Rome's main airport is **Leonardo da Vinci** (1, A2; ☎ 06 659 55 571; www.adr.it), commonly referred to as Fiumicino, 30km southwest of the city. Arrivals use the ground floor, departures the 1st. Facilities include banks, exchange booths (close midnight), post offices and shops.

Airport Access
Train Two trains connect Fiumicino to the city. The Leonardo Express runs every 30 minutes from 5.52am to 10.52pm (from Termini) and 6.37am to 11.37pm (from Fiumicino). The trip takes 30 minutes and costs €9.50 one way (€11 if you buy the ticket on board). The other train (a local service) is more frequent, stopping at Trastevere (25 minutes), Ostiense (30 minutes) and Tiburtina (40 minutes) stations but not at Termini. From the airport, these slower trains run about every 20 minutes (€5 one way). Tickets for both trains can be bought from vending machines in the main airport arrivals hall (credit's the easiest way to go), from ticket offices, newspaper shops or vending machines at train stations.

Bus Bus company **Cotral** (☎ 800 15 00 08; www.cotralspa.it) operates a nightbus from Fiumicino to Termini and Tiburtina stations, approx every hour from 11.30pm to 6am (€5 one way) to the airport, and 1.15am to 5am to the city.

Taxi A taxi (use only the yellow or white licensed ones) from Fiumicino to the centre takes at least 45 minutes and costs from €40 to €60 (including airport supplement).

CIAMPINO
Many discount airlines and charter flights operate out of the much smaller and less-convenient **Ciampino airport** (1, B2; ☎ 06 794 94 225; www.adr.it), 15km southeast of the centre.

Airport Access
Bus From Ciampino, take the Cotral bus to Anagnina (€1, every 60 to 90 minutes), then the metro to your destination. A combined trip takes one to 2½ hours depending on your luck with the connections. Buy your ticket from the newspaper shop inside the airport. Alternatively take a Cotral or a **Shiaffini** (www.shiaffini.com) bus to Ciampino train station from where you can take a train to Termini (€1.70).

Taxi A taxi trip takes at least 45 minutes and costs around €45 (plus luggage supplements).

Train
Stazione Termini (5, B3) is Rome's main train hub, although some trains serve Tiburtina (3, F3). There are regular trains to other European destinations as well as major cities and smaller towns in Italy. For information go to the busy offices of **Trenitalia**

(☎ 1478 880 88, Italian only; www.tren italia.com; ⏲ 7am-9pm & 7am-9.45pm) next to platforms 5 and 22 at Termini.

Bus
Cotral (☎ 800 431 784; www.atac.roma .it) buses operate right throughout the Lazio region and depart from several points (usually metro stations), heading in different directions.

Eurolines (☎ 055 357 110; www.euro lines.com) is the main carrier for all European destinations, and is connected with coach operators throughout Europe. Buses leave from Stazione Tiburtina.

Travel Documents
PASSPORT
If you need a visa for entry to Italy, your passport will have to be valid for several months after the date of entry.

VISA
European Union (EU) citizens only need to bring a passport or ID card. Nationals of Australia, Canada, Japan, New Zealand and the USA do not need a visa for up to three months if entering as tourists. Other nationals and those who wish to stay for lengthy periods or for work or study purposes should check with their local Italian embassy.

Customs & Duty Free
Goods brought in and exported within the EU incur no additional taxes. This is provided that duty has been paid somewhere within the EU and the goods are for personal consumption.

Non-EU nationals can import/export 200 cigarettes, 1L of spirits, 2L wine, 60mL perfume, 250mL eau de toilette and other goods up to a total of €180 duty free; anything over this limit should be declared on arrival and the appropriate duty paid.

Departure Tax
Don't sweat, airport taxes are included in the price of your ticket.

Left Luggage
Luggage can be left at the arrivals area of Fiumicino (per day €3.50) airport only. At Stazione Termini, the left luggage deposit is under platform 24 (for 5 hours €3.80, per hour between 6 and 12 hours €0.60, from 13 hours €0.20).

GETTING AROUND
Rome's buses, trams, subway (Metropolitana) and suburban railways are part of an integrated system run by ATAC. For information on fares and routes call ☎ 800 431 784 or see www.atac.roma.it.

Tickets must be purchased in advance and validated as you get onto the bus/tram or enter the platform. You won't see them very often but if an inspector does catch you without a validated ticket, no excuse will get you out of €52 fine.

Children under 1m tall travel free on public transport.

Travel Passes
ATAC's *biglietti integrati* is valid for all modes of transport within the metropolitan area: €1/4/11/16 per 75 minutes/day/3 days/ week. You can buy tickets from local tobacconists, newsstands and from the vending machines at metro stations and main bus stops.

Separate tickets are required for Cotral bus travel outside the metropolitan area. Daily regional tickets, which are known as BIRG, are useful for travel on the ATAC metropolitan network, FS trains and Cotral buses; they are generally available only from bus termini/metro stations.

Bus & Tram
Many of the main ATAC bus routes terminate in Piazza dei Cinquecento at Stazione Termini. Other useful bus hubs are Piazza Venezia, Largo Argentina and Piazza San Silvestro. Night buses cover some routes, running from 12.30am to 5.30am from Piazza dei Cinquecento and the other main

bus termini. Bus and tram maps can be bought from newsstands or are free from the **ATAC office** (17 Via Gaeta; ☺ 7am-6.45pm).

There are signs at each stop listing the streets and piazzas the route serves. For the sights, shops and restaurants etc listed throughout this guide, we've suggested the closest main street or piazza to aim for (unless there's only one service, in which case we've provided the number).

Metropolitana

The two-line **Metro** (www.metroroma.it) seems to be always packed and operates from 5.30am to 11.30pm (to 12.30am Saturday) with trains running every five to 10 minutes. Both lines, A and B, pass through Stazione Termini. Line A is currently undergoing construction work until 2008, and closes at 9pm.

Train

Ferrovia metropolitana (suburban trains) are operated by Ferrovie dello Stato (FS). ATAC Metrebus tickets are valid for journeys within the metropolitan area.

Taxi

Rome's taxis are relatively expensive. Flag-fall during the day/after 10pm/Sunday is €2.33/4.91/3.36 (for the first 3km), then €0.65 per km with supplements for luggage at €1.05 per item. Pick one up from a taxi rank, hail one on the street (although officially not allowed) or call ☎ 06 55 51, ☎ 06 49 94 or ☎ 06 35 70 (but be aware that the meter starts running as soon as you book).

Car & Motorcycle

Do you really want to take 10 years off your life? Driving in Rome is a complete nightmare. Only residents with permits can enter the *centro storico* (historic city centre), although tourists are sometimes permitted to drive to their hotels, streets are badly signposted with a complicated one-way

system, parking is difficult and/or expensive, and Roman drivers are completely bonkers. *Motorini* (scooters) can enter the *centro storico* and are a fast way to get around and will make you feel like you're in *Roman Holiday* – but bear in mind that drivers are mad, roads are bumpy and busy and many Romans come a cropper despite their *motorini* know-how.

ROAD RULES

What road rules? Well, there are some: Italians drive on the right. Seatbelts are compulsory (hmph!) and speed limits are technically 50km/h in built-up areas, 90km/h on country roads, 110km/h on main roads/highways and 130km/h on motorways. The blood-alcohol limit when driving is 0.08%.

HIRE

You will probably only need a car for excursions out of Rome. Average rental cars cost from €65 per day; good 3-day weekend deals are available. Main companies include **Avis** (☎ 06 452 10 83 91; www.avis.com), **Europcar** (☎ 02 703 99 700; www.europcar.com) and **Maggiore Nutional** (☎ 848 86 70 67; www.maggiore.it), all of which have outlets at Fiumicino and Termini. Scooters cost around €15 to €25 per day to hire.

DRIVING LICENCE & PERMITS

If you are planning on driving, bring an EU driving licence or an International Driving Permit plus your home-country licence.

PRACTICAL INFORMATION
Business Hours

Banks (☺ 8.30am-1.30pm & 2.45-4.30pm Mon-Fri; some central banks also 9am-12.30pm Sat)

Shops (☺ 9am-1pm & 3.30-7.30pm Mon-Sat; some stay open all day, close Thu pm and/or open Sun)

Offices (☺ 9am-1.30pm & 4-7.30pm Mon-Fri; some also 9am-1.30pm Sat)

Climate & When to Go

Rome is a city for all seasons. April to May and September to October are ideal weather-wise (though November is often rainy), and the high seasons for tourists, so accommodation can be scarce. From late June to August it's hot and humid, sometimes unbearably so, but this is when Rome is most vibrant, with life spilling onto the streets and open-air festivals in abundance. It can be cold from December to February, but the days are more often than not bright and sunny.

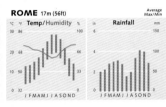

ROME 17m (56ft)

Disabled Travellers

Rome is not an easy city for disabled travellers – with cobbled, narrow streets and cars frequently parked across the pavements, getting around can be a problem for the mobility impaired. However, wheelchair-accessible buses have been introduced on many busy ATAC bus routes and Rome's newer trams are accessible. Most of Metro line B is wheelchair-accessible, but line A is not, though bus 590 is wheelchair accessible and follows the same route.

You can call ahead for assistance at Stazione Termini (☎ 06 488 17 26) and Fiumcino Airport (☎ 06 650 11 821).

Although many buildings have lifts, they are often too narrow to accommodate a wheelchair. Some taxis are equipped to carry passengers in wheelchairs; it is advisable to book these by phone, and ask for one suitable for a *sedia a rotelle*. Things are looking better now for disabled travellers than ever before as many museums' facilities have been updated over recent years.

Braille labels are being introduced in some museums, as are special audio guides for the hearing impaired, but there's a long way to go.

INFORMATION & ORGANISATIONS

COIN (☎ 06 232 69 231; www.coinsociale.it) This is a proactive organisation which assists disabled tourists; its free publication *Roma Accessible* is available by phone order or online.

Discounts

Children under 18 and seniors over 65 get free entry to all state and city museums, and discounted admission to private museums and sights. Card-carrying students and teachers and those aged 18 to 25 get *prezzo ridotto* (reduced admission) to most museums and sights.

STUDENT & YOUTH CARDS

The International Student Identity Card (ISIC) is the most widely accepted form of student identification.

Electricity

Cycle AC
Frequency 50Hz
Plugs Two or three round pins.
Voltage 220V

Embassies & Consulates

Australia (3, D3; ☎ 06 852 721; www.italy.embassy.gov.au; Via Antonio Bosio 5)
Canada (3, E3; ☎ 06 445 981; www.canada.it; Via G B de Rossi 27)
New Zealand (3, D3; ☎ 06 441 7171; www.nzembassy.com; Via Zara 28)
South Africa (3, D2; ☎ 06 852 541; www.sudafrica.it; Via Tanaro 14)
UK (5, B1; ☎ 06 422 00 001; www.britishembassy.gov.uk; Via XX Settembre 80a)
USA (4, H2; ☎ 06 467 41; www.usis.it; Via Vittorio Veneto 119a-121)

Emergencies

Ambulance (☎ 118)
Fire (☎ 115)
Police (☎ 113)

Fitness

Romans love sport although they're not especially keen on taking part. You'll get plenty of exercise walking between the sights, striding towards views and trying to cross roads, but opportunities to get your endorphins pumping are largely limited to a few gyms, pools (see Roman Indulgence, p43) or a run around the city's parks – Villa Doria Pamphilj (3, A5) is a particularly popular place to jog.

Rome's largest and best-equipped gym, **Roman Sport Center** (4, G1; ☎ 06 320 16 67; www.romansportcenter.com; Viale del Galoppatoio 33; day pass €27; ☼ 8am-10pm Mon-Sat, 9am-3pm Sun Oct-May), has two Olympic-sized pools, saunas, sun beds, squash courts and all the weights and cardio machines you could ever need. It's closed in summer. Enter from Spagna metro.

Gay & Lesbian Travellers

Despite the Vatican's periodic anti-gay diatribes, homosexuality is legal in Italy (the legal age of consent is 16) and well tolerated in Rome, though open displays of affection are best preserved for more liberated nations. Previously a subculture that operated behind closed doors, Rome's gay scene is now a lot more open, if not overt, and there are numerous bars and clubs, with new venues opening regularly. For more information see p94.

There is no centre for gay life, although there are a number of bars and saunas around the Monti/Esquiline areas.

INFORMATION & ORGANISATIONS

The hub of Rome's gay and lesbian activity is the **Circolo Mario Mieli di Cultura Omosessuale** (3, B7; ☎ 06 541 39 85; www.mariomieli.it, Italian only; Via Efeso 2a). The **Coordinamento Lesbiche Italiano** (4, C5; ☎ 06 686 42 01; www.clrbp.it; Via di San Francesco di Sales 1), also known as Buon Pastore Centre, has regular political gatherings and social events for lesbians.

Other useful sources of information include *Pride* (€3.10) a national monthly magazine, international gay guide *Spartacus*, and online www.gay.it/guida/Lazio/Roma (Italian only) with listings for Rome and Lazio, or www.gayroma.com.

Health
IMMUNISATIONS

There are no vaccination requirements for entry to Italy.

PRECAUTIONS

Rome's tap water is safe to drink (although it contains a lot of calcium and many people prefer to drink the bottled stuff) and food preparation is fairly hygienic. It's advisable to wash fruit bought from markets. Heat and humidity are the only things likely to get you down; wear a hat and loose comfortable clothing and drink plenty of fluids.

INSURANCE & MEDICAL TREATMENT

Travel insurance is advisable to cover any medical treatment you may need while in Rome. However, all foreigners have the same right as locals to emergency or essential medical treatment, including ongoing treatment, in a public hospital or clinic.

Citizens of EU countries should have a European Health Insurance Card (EHIC). This has replaced the E111 form since 1 January 2006, and entitles you to free or reduced-cost medical treatment in Italy. It's usually simplest to apply for a card online via your National Health Authority (www.dh.gov.uk in the UK), who also supply details of what the card covers.

MEDICAL SERVICES

The emergency number is ☎ 118. Hospitals with 24 hour accident and emergency departments:
Ospedale Bambino Gesù (4, B4; ☎ 06 682 77; Piazza Sant'Onofrio) For children.
Ospedale Fatebenefratelli (2, B2; ☎ 06 335 81; Piazza Fatebenefratelli)

Ospedale San Giacomo (4, E2; ☎ 06 362 61; Via A Canova 29)
Policlinico Umberto I (5, C2; ☎ 06 499 71; Viale del Policlinico 155)

DENTAL SERVICES
If you chip a tooth or require emergency treatment, head to **Ospedale di Odonto-iatria** (3, E3; ☎ 06 84 48 31; Viale Regina Elena 287b).

PHARMACIES
Farmacie are usually open Monday to Saturday 9am to 1pm and 4pm to 7.30pm. They open after hours on a rotation basis. Night pharmacies are listed in the daily newspapers. When closed, pharmacies display a list of others open nearby. There's a 24-hour pharmacy at Piazza Cinquecento 51 (5, B3; ☎ 06 488 00 19) and one inside Stazione Termini (5, B3; lower ground floor) that is open from 7am to 10pm.

Holidays
New Year's Day 1 January
Epiphany 6 January
Easter Monday March/April
Liberation Day 25 April
Labour Day 1 May
Feast of SS Peter & Paul 29 June
Ferragosto (Feast of the Assumption) 15 August
All Saints' Day 1 November
Christmas Day 25 December
Santo Stefan (Boxing Day) 26 December

Internet
If you packed your laptop, note that Italy uses a three-pin phone plug that accommodates a US or French-style jack. Newer plugs (including modern plugs in many hotels) take the jack directly into the wall.

Many upmarket hotels, and even a few budget ones, offer wi-fi, but the most spectacular place to access your mail is Villa Borghese (see p13), which has a number of open-air wi-fi hotspots – the various locations are given at the park entrances.

INTERNET CAFÉS
If you can't access the Internet from where you're staying, then maybe you should head to one of the following cybercafés:
Bibli (2, A2; ☎ 06 588 40 97; www.bibli .it, Italian only; Via dei Fienaroli 28; per hr €3.50; ⊙ 11am-midnight)
easyInternetcafé (4, H3; www.easyInter netcafe.com; Via Barberini 2; per hr €2; ⊙ 8am-2am)
Pantheon Internet (6, D3; ☎ 06 6920 0501; Via Santa Caterina 48; per hr €4.15; ⊙ 10am-8pm) Wi-fi hotspot.

USEFUL WEBSITES
The Lonely Planet website (www.lonely planet.com) offers a speedy link to many of Rome's websites. Others to try include the following:
Comune di Roma (www.roma turismo.it)
Enjoy Rome (www.enjoyrome.com) Tourist office and travel agent.
In Rome Now (www.inromenow.com)
Museums in Italy (www.museionline.it)
Vatican (www.vatican.va)
Wanted in Rome (www.wantedinrome .com)
What's on in Rome (www .whatsoninrome.com)

Lost Property
For items lost on a bus call ☎ 06 581 60 40, on the metro call ☎ 06 487 43 09 (Line A) or ☎ 06 575 32 265 and on a train ☎ 06 473 06 682.

Metric System
The metric system is standard. Like other Continental Europeans, Italians use commas in decimals, and points to indicate thousands.

Money
CURRENCY
With the lira long gone, Italy – like most of the EU – deals in euros, which comes in piddling coinage 1, 2, 5, 10, 20, 50 cents, €1

and €2 coins, and €5, €10, €20, €50, €100, €200 and €500 notes.

TRAVELLERS CHEQUES

Travellers cheques can be cashed at any bank or exchange office, such as **American Express** (4, G2; ☎ 06 6 76 41; Piazza di Spagna 38; 🕘 9am-5.30pm Mon-Fri, 9am-12.30pm Sat). Call toll-free ☎ 800 872 000 for lost cheques.

CREDIT CARDS

Major credit cards, such as Amex, Visa, MasterCard, Eurocard, Cirrus and Euro Cheques, are accepted throughout Rome although many smaller hotels, restaurants and shops do not accept them. Diners Club and JCB are accepted less frequently. Credit cards can also be used in ATMs displaying the appropriate sign. For 24 hour card cancellations or assistance, call

American Express (☎ 06 7 22 82)
MasterCard (☎ 800 870 866)
Visa (☎ 800 877 232)

ATMS

Automatic Teller Machines can be found outside most banks, in the airport halls and at Stazione Termini. Visa and Mastercard/Eurocard are widely accepted, as well as cash cards that access the Cirrus/Maestro network.

CHANGING MONEY

Banks generally offer better rates than *cambi* (bureaux de change) although commissions can vary – anything from €1 to a hefty percentage of the amount exchanged. Exchange bureaux are open longer hours than banks so you're paying for convenience. Don't forget to bring your passport or photo ID.

Newspapers & Magazines

Il Messaggero is Rome's most popular broadsheet, with a weekly listings supplement, *Metro*. *La Repubblica* is moderately left-wing and has an excellent listings guide, *Trovaroma*, every Thursday. Milan-based *Corriere della Sera* (articles in English are available on the website www.corriere.it/english/) is the country's leading broadsheet. The conservative daily *L'Osservatore Romano*, the official voice of the Vatican, has weekly editions in English and other foreign languages.

The *International Herald Tribune* (Monday to Saturday) has a supplement on Italian news, *Italy Daily*. Major British and US daily papers and weekly news magazines are the available same (or next) day from larger newsstands; the bigger and more central the newsstand, the more recent the edition.

Roma C'é (€1.20) comes out every Wednesday and has a section in English at the back.

Photography

Print and slide film and digital memory cards are available from photo shops and some supermarkets. There are plenty of photo shops that sell camera gear and do repairs, and will put your photos onto CD. You can also print (€2 per print) or download pictures onto CD (€5) at easyInternet-café (opposite).

Post

Italian post is notoriously unreliable and parcels often go missing, though letters and your postcards home are pretty safe, sent via the speedier, more efficient *posta prioritaria* service. Stamps are sold at post office counters and most tobacconists. The Vatican post is more efficient and reliable – note that you need Vatican stamps to use it (there are post offices in the Vatican museums and next to St Peter's).

Local post offices usually open 8.30am to 1.50pm Monday to Friday and 8.30am to 11.50am Saturday. All post offices close two hours earlier than normal on the last business day of the month.

Main post office (4, F3; Piazza di San Silvestro 18-20; 🕘 8.30am-6.30pm Mon-Fri, 8.30am-1pm Sat)

POSTAL RATES

The world is divided into three zones: Zone 1 (Europe and the Mediterranean Basin), Zone 2 (other African countries, Asia and the Americas), and Zone 3 (the Pacific, including Australia, Japan and New Zealand). Postcards and letters (up to 20g) sent *posta prioritaria* cost €0.62/0.80/1. Registered mail costs €2.80/3/3.05 on top. You can insure an item up to a value of €50 for €5.30/5.50/5.55.

Radio

There are three state-owned stations: RAI-1 (1332AM or 89.7FM), RAI-2 (846AM or 91.7FM) and RAI-3 (93.7FM). They combine classical and light music with news broadcasts and discussion programmes.

Commercial radio stations are a better bet if you're after contemporary music. Try Radio Centro Suono (101.3FM) or the excellent Radio Città Futura (97.7FM), which broadcasts a listing of the day's events in Rome at 10am, and the news from the BBC World Service at 10pm.

You can pick up the BBC World Service on medium wave at 648kHz, short wave at 6195kHz, 9410kHz, 12095kHz, 15575kHz and on long wave at 198kHz, depending on where you are and the time of day.

Telephone

A *comunicazione urbana* (local call) from a public phone will cost around €0.20 for 3 to 6 minutes, depending on the time of day. Phone booths are operated by Telecom Italia, Infostrada and Albacom; each needs its own dedicated phonecard. A few phone booths also take coins. There are also lots of cut-price call centres – rates at these are lower for international calls (you can also use them for domestic calls). You place your call in a booth and pay afterwards.

PHONECARDS

Phonecards are available in €5/10/20 denominations; they can be bought from post offices, tobacconists and some newsstands.

They can be used for both local and international calls.

MOBILE PHONES

Italy uses the GSM cellular phone system, compatible with phones sold in the UK, Australia and most of Asia, but not those from North American or Japan. Check with your mobile phone company before you leave home that they have a roaming agreement with a local counterpart.

COUNTRY & CITY CODES
Italy (☎ 39)
Rome (☎ 06)

The first 0 is an integral part of Roman phone numbers and is retained wherever you're calling from. However, when calling an Italian mobile from outside the country, drop the 0 after the country code.

USEFUL NUMBERS
Directory Inquiries (☎ 412)
International Directory Inquiries (☎ 4176)
Reverse-Charge (collect) (☎ 170)

Television

Italian TV is compellingly bad, with an inordinate number of quiz shows, reality shows, cleavage, impassioned ballads and men in drag. It does show lots of recent films, all dubbed into Italian.

There are seven major networks; the state-run channels RAI 1, RAI 2 and RAI 3 and commercial stations Canale 5, Italia 1, Rete 4 owned by former Prime Minister and now leader of the opposition Silvio Berlusconi (hang on! Isn't that?...best not to ask) and the third-ranking La Sette. Most of Rome's mid- to top-range hotels, as well as many bars and restaurants, have satellite TV and can receive BBC World, Sky Channel, CNN and NBC.

Time

Rome Standard Time is 1 hour ahead of GMT. Daylight savings time is practised from the last Sunday in March to the last Sunday in October.

Tipping
In restaurants where service is not included it's customary to leave a 10% tip; if service is included, you don't have to leave anything. Tipping taxi drivers is not common practice, but at upmarket hotels you should cross the porter's hand with silver.

Toilets
Public toilets are scarce. Most people use the toilets in bars and cafés – although you might need to buy a coffee first and they won't necessarily be clean or have toilet paper.

Stazione Termini's public toilets are on the lower ground level (€0.70; ☼ 6am-midnight).

Tourist Information
LOCAL TOURIST INFORMATION
There's an information office run by the Comune di Roma at Stazione Termini, next to Platform 24 (8.15am to 7pm). Free city maps and brochures on museums, festivals and events are available. **Comune tourism infoline** (☎ 06 820 59 127; www.comune .roma.it) operates 9am to 7.30pm.

There are 10 comune tourist information kiosks dotted around the city, open from 9am to 7.30pm daily: Piazza dei Cinquecento (5, B3); Via dei Fori Imperiali (4, H5); Via Nazionale (4, H3); Via del Corso at Via Minghetti (6, E1); Via del Corso at Largo Goldoni (4, F2); Castel Sant'Angelo (4, C3); Trastevere (2, A2); Piazza di Santa Maria Maggiore (5, A4); Piazza Cinque Lune (6, B1); Piazza San Giovanni in Laterano (3, D5).

The **Azienda di Promozione Turistica** (APT; 5, A2; ☎ 06 488 99 212; www.roma turismo.it; Via Parigi 5; ☼ 9am-7pm Mon-Sat) is run by the regional authorities and has information on destinations outside the city centre. There's another office (☼ 8.15pm-7pm) at Terminal B, Fiumicino airport.

Women Travellers
Rome is not a dangerous city for women, but women travelling alone will often find themselves plagued by unwanted male attention, especially in bars and clubs. Be careful which venues you frequent after dark, and particularly when leaving them. Avoid walking alone in dark and deserted streets, and look to stay in a central hotel, close to the restaurants and bars you'll be frequenting.

Beware of men with wandering hands on crowded buses (especially the No 64). A loud *cheschifo*! (how disgusting!) usually does the trick.

Tampons (and more commonly, sanitary pads) are available in pharmacies and supermarkets.

Language
Italian is a Romance language related to French, Spanish, Portuguese and Romanian. As English and Italian share common roots in Latin, you'll more than likely recognise many Italian words.

The Roman accent is quite harsh. Like all other regions of Italy, Romans have their own Italian dialect and slang.

Many Italians speak at least some English because they study it at school. Staff at many hotels and restaurants often speak a little English, but you will be better received if you at least attempt to communicate in Italian.

Here are some useful phrases that will get you started. Grab a copy of Lonely Planet's *Italian Phrasebook* if you'd like to know more.

Basics

Hello. (morning)	Buongiorno. (pol)
Hello. (afternoon/ evening)	Buonasera. (pol)
Hi.	Ciao. (inf)
Goodbye.	Arrivederci. (pol)
	Ciao. (inf)
Yes.	Sì.
No.	No.

Please.	Per favore/Per piacere.
Thank you.	Grazie.
You're welcome.	Prego.
Excuse me.	Mi scusi.
Sorry (forgive me).	Mi perdoni/ Mi dispiace.
Do you speak English?	Parla inglese?
I don't understand.	Non capisco.
How much is it?	Quanto costa?

Getting Around

When does the ... leave/arrive?	A che ora parte/arriva ...?
bus	l'autobus
train	il treno
I'd like a ... ticket.	Vorrei un biglietto di ...
one-way	solo andata
return	andata e ritorno
left luggage	deposito bagagli
Where is ...?	Dov'è ... ?
Go straight ahead.	Si va sempre diritto.
Turn left/right.	Giri a sinistra/destra.

Around Town

I'm looking for ...	Cerco ...
a bank	una banca
chemist/pharmacy	la farmacia
the tourist office	l'ufficio di turismo
What time does it open/close?	A che ora (si) apre/chiude?

Accommodation

a hotel	un albergo
Do you have any rooms available?	Avete delle camere libere?
a ... room	una camera ...
single	singola
twin	doppia
double	matrimoniale
a room with bathroom	una camera con bagno

Eating

breakfast	colazione
lunch	pranzo
dinner	cena
The bill, please.	Il conto, per favore.
I'm a vegetarian.	Sono vegetariano/a.

Shopping

I'm just looking.	Sto solo guardando.
How much is it?	Quanto costa?
Do you accept... ?	Accettate... ?
credit cards	carte di credito
travellers cheques	assegni per viaggiatori

Time, Days & Numbers

What time is it?	Che ora è?
It's one o'clock.	È l'una.
It's two thirty.	Sono le due e mezza.
today	oggi
tomorrow	domani
yesterday	ieri
morning	mattina
afternoon	pomeriggio
day	giorno
hour	ora
Monday	lunedì
Tuesday	martedì
Wednesday	mercoledì
Thursday	giovedì
Friday	venerdì
Saturday	sabato
Sunday	domenica
1	uno
2	due
3	tre
4	quattro
5	cinque
6	sei
7	sette
8	otto
9	nove
10	dieci
100	cento
1000	mille

Index

SLEEPING

FEATURES

La Rosetta	*Eating*
Teatro Olimpico	*Entertainment*
Bar della Pace	*Drinking*
Tre Scalini	*Café*
Colosseum	*Highlights*
Gianni Versace	*Shopping*
Fontana di Trevi	*Sights/Activities*
Hotel Modigliani	*Sleeping*
Ostia Antica	*Trips & Tours*

AREAS

	Beach, Desert
	Building
	Land
	Mall
	Other Area
	Park/Cemetery
	Sports
	Urban

HYDROGRAPHY

	River, Creek
	Intermittent River
	Canal
	Swamp
	Water

BOUNDARIES

	State, Provincial
	Regional, Suburb

ROUTES

	Tollway
	Freeway
	Primary Road
	Secondary Road
	Tertiary Road
	Lane
	Under Construction
	One-Way Street
	Unsealed Road
	Mall/Steps
	Tunnel
	Walking Path
	Walking Trail/Track
	Pedestrian Overpass
	Walking Tour

TRANSPORT

	Airport, Airfield
	Bus Route
	Cycling, Bicycle Path
	Ferry
	General Transport
	Metro
	Monorail
	Rail
	Taxi Rank
	Tram

SYMBOLS

	Bank, ATM
	Buddhist
	Castle, Fortress
	Christian
	Diving, Snorkelling
	Embassy, Consulate
	Hospital, Clinic
	Information
	Internet Access
	Islamic
	Jewish
	Lighthouse
	Lookout
	Monument
	Mountain, Volcano
	National Park
	Parking Area
	Petrol Station
	Picnic Area
	Point of Interest
	Police Station
	Post Office
	Ruin
	Telephone
	Toilets
	Waterfall
	Zoo, Bird Sanctuary

24/7 travel advice
www.lonelyplanet.com